Oswin Craton has done it again! Reading *Orthodox Saints of Wales* was like being introduced to a branch of the family that I knew existed but had never actually met. While their names seem unusual, their Christian spirit is warmly familiar. What a joy to meet our Welsh cousins in the Faith!

—V. Rev. Fr. Peter Jon Gillquist, All Saints Antiochian Orthodox Church in Bloomington, Indiana

Orthodox Saints of Wales is a straightforward and enjoyable gallery of the holy men and women who shaped the Faith of the Celtic world in the great Age of Saints. With a sense of devotion and a love for the ancient British saints, it is an Orthodox celebration of their spiritual labours and power, reflecting their kinship, interconnectedness, and friendships through the short biographies that open their lives and spiritual world to the Orthodox reader today, showing a Christian society united in living Faith and the struggle for holiness.

—Hieromonk Mark Underwood, Parish of the Kazan Icon of the Mother of God, Cardiff

Oswin Craton covers in a chronological and detailed way the lives of the saints of Wales over seven centuries, with miracles and stories that are hard to believe. So many of the lives are those of young people, and today's youth will enjoy the witness to Christ and stories of sacrifice and miracles. The challenges to these saints came from the pagan Saxons, King Henry VIII, and others who also destroyed churches and monasteries, along with their records, so that some details of Orthodox saints in these centuries were lost along with the faithful saints themselves. The book is an education in history, spirituality, and life in Wales over the centuries. For one who knew nothing about Orthodox saints from Wales, I was blessed to have read it.

—Fr. Seraphim Moslener, pastor of St. John the Evangelist Antiochian Orthodox Church in Beaver Falls, Pennsylvania

ORTHODOX
SAINTS OF WALES

OSWIN CRATON

Illustrations by Mark Ari Fisher

ANCIENT FAITH PUBLISHING
CHESTERTON, INDIANA

Published by:
Ancient Faith Publishing
A Division of Ancient Faith Ministries
1050 Broadway, Suite 6
Chesterton, IN 46304

Cover art by Mark Ari Fisher

ISBN: 978-1-955890-77-9

Library of Congress Control Number: 2025936794

CONTENTS

Golden Age of Saints

ACKNOWLEDGMENTS

I WISH TO GIVE SPECIAL THANKS to Fr. Timothy Pearce, pastor of the Orthodox Community of the Three Holy Hierarchs in Cardiganshire, for his assistance in the preparation of this book, and notably for introducing me to his chief cantor, Hellier Johns. Mr. Johns has been an invaluable source of guidance and encouragement throughout this process and has freely offered his time and expertise to provide much-needed input in regards particularly to geographical locations and the Welsh language. Being several thousand miles removed and with only the most tenuous knowledge of Welsh, I simply could not have completed this book without his generous help and insight.

Thanks also to the Members of Wales Orthodox Mission, who provided further help with the Welsh language during the illustration process.

INTRODUCTION

WHEN ST. GREGORY THE GREAT sent St. Augustine of Canterbury to evangelize England, Christianity was already long established in parts of what is now Wales, though no one knows who first brought it there. Around the year 200, Tertullian mentioned in his *Adversus Judaeus* that he had heard of places in Britain that had been won for Christ, though he offered no details.[1] It is possible that Christians fleeing from the persecution in Lyons in 177 fled to Britain, carrying the gospel with them. J. B. Davies contends that this Lyons connection seems likely[2] and would explain why the Celtic church was more Eastern in character than the church in Continental Europe, which was more influenced by Rome.

According to some early accounts, a first-century king of Britain, St. Cyllin, became a Christian, together with his sister St. Eigen— and the two were the first Christians in Wales.[3] A listing of the Seventy Apostles (Luke 10:1) by Pseudo-Hippolytus of Thebes names St. Aristobulus as bishop of Britain, perhaps as early as mid-first century.[4] Other ancient sources, such as William of Malmesbury's *De Antiquitate Glastoniensis Ecclesiae,* claim that St. Ilid arrived in Wales

---

1   Tertullian, *Complete Works,* chap. 7.
2   J. B. Davies, *Saints of Wales,* 1.
3   Richard Morgan, *St. Paul in Britain,* 161.
4   Burke, "List of the Apostles and Disciples."

1

in the late first century, and as "a man of Israel" (i.e., one born Jewish) he actually may have been Joseph of Arimathea.[5]

In his *Histories of the Kings of Britain*,[6] Geoffrey of Monmouth said that Ss. Ffagan and Deruvian were second-century missionaries to Wales, though some historians argue that Geoffrey's accounts are less than reliable. Others suggest that St. Tyfanog came to preach the gospel in Wales in 186 and was martyred on Ramsey Island, though the hagiographer Sabine Baring-Gould mentions only that St. Tyfanog was listed on a thirteenth-century menology and that a chapel on Ramsey Island was dedicated to him.[7] Beyond that he admits that "Who this . . . Tyfanog was it is impossible to say."[8]

The names of two other early Welsh martyrs also survive (Aaron and Julian of Caerleon), who were martyred around the year 300.[9] Saint Gildas, writing in the sixth century, tells us that many other Christians "stood firm in Christ's army," but he laments that their graves no longer could be venerated since their locations had been lost after being overrun by the pagan Saxon invaders.[10] But whoever was the first to bring the good news of Christ to the island, Christianity had a significant presence in Wales, beginning at least in the late first century. Because of this, when Christianity became the official religion of Rome in the fourth century, it was already firmly entrenched in Wales. Being somewhat isolated from the rest of Europe (even from the rest of Britain) by the Saxon and Angle invasions, the church in Wales retained more of its distinctive Celtic/ Orthodox character than other churches in the West.

---

5   Griffin, *Glastonbury and the Grail*, 96–97.
6   Geoffrey of Monmouth, *Histories*, bk. 4, chap. 9.
7   Baring-Gould, *Lives of the British Saints*, vol. 4, 290–291.
8   Baring-Gould and Fisher, *Lives of the British Saints*, vol. 2, 395.
9   Hutchison-Hall, *Orthodox Saints*, vol. 3, 21.
10 J. B. Davies, 1.

The fifth, sixth, and seventh centuries saw a flourishing of faith in the land, and these centuries became known as the "Golden Age of Saints" in Wales. Regrettably, however, in many cases only the names of these saints are known with any degree of credibility, and what little remains known of their lives has been handed down mostly in fragments.

Why Do We Have So Little Information About These Saints?

It is probable that local monasteries kept detailed hagiographies that carefully preserved the lives and deeds of these saints during and shortly after they lived, but time and history worked against the preservation of these cherished documents. Aside from the ordinary ravages of time, such as the fires and floods that likely consumed many ancient monastic texts, there were also threats of more human origins that played a major role in the loss of information. The fate of St. Beuno's famous monastery at Clynnog Fawr serves as one example of this. Like most buildings in Wales of that time, the monastery and abbey church were built not of stone but of wood.[11] They all were burned to the ground by Vikings in 978, and after being rebuilt they were again completely destroyed by the Normans a century later.[12] Additionally, a number of Welsh monasteries lay near the coasts, where they were susceptible to frequent raids by pirates, who would loot and destroy many of these texts.

Hence the very early records of saints' lives we have today are generally reconstructed from fragmentary records or from local folklore that was often embellished during the later medieval period after Rome subsumed the more Orthodox Celtic Christianity in Wales

---

11   Gerald Morgan, 34.
12   Lapa, "Venerable Beuno."

following the Norman Conquest of 1066. During the Conquest, William the Conqueror invaded England with the pope's blessing and began introducing a Norman influence on Christianity throughout Britain, bringing it more into subjection to Rome than it had been previously. By the 1090s this Norman control had reached into Wales and reformed much of the Celtic church there,[13] bringing in new orders of monks and placing Norman priests and bishops in positions of oversight.[14]

Of the monastic libraries that survived the Middle Ages, most were destroyed during the Reformation when King Henry VIII implemented the dissolution of all monasteries in the sixteenth century.[15] When he closed all monasteries and confiscated their valuables, his agents also seized, redistributed, burned, or otherwise destroyed entire libraries.[16] What happened at St. Davids, one of the most important religious and intellectual centers of Wales, was typical: When the first Protestant bishop arrived in 1550, he burned all manuscripts he could find. The church sexton had hidden other manuscripts, but when they were discovered in 1571, they were "torn to pieces in the Vestrie before his face."[17] It is impossible to know the full extent of what was lost during this turbulent period, but the impressive number of accounts of relics, religious art, and church documents that were confiscated and subsequently mislaid or deliberately destroyed certainly goes far to explain why source material is significantly limited.

Because of all of this, it is difficult to separate historical fact from local legend when it comes to information about the lives of these saints, and since nearly all contemporaneous sources have been lost

---

13   Jones et al., *A History of Christianity in Wales,* 97 ff.
14   Gerald Morgan, 44–45.
15   Clark, *Dissolution of the Monasteries,* 778–782.
16   Lewis, "Lost Literature."
17   J. B. Davies, 17.

the hagiographies presented in this book reflect what information has been passed down anecdotally. Some post-Schism embellishment of certain of these lives seems likely, given that different accounts record markedly different events, but it is not our place to stand in judgment of their authenticity but rather to record for posterity the holy character of these beloved saints and the acts for which they are still known and revered today. Where ancient records give divergent accounts of various lives, I have presented here what seems the most feasible among them.

The reader also will notice inconsistencies between dates in these biographies. We simply do not know exact dates for many of these saints, as the records have been lost over time. Even our best guesses often cannot account for certain contradictions, such as some saints interacting with others apparently years before one or the other of them was born. Again, I resort frequently to a "best guess" approximation when presenting chronological data.

Even the century with which a particular saint is associated may sometimes be in question, in part because of the lack of evidence and also because several saints were born and lived much of their lives in one century but died in the next. Generally, saints are assigned to the century in which they reposed, though this is not always the case.

Monasticism in Early Wales

Many of these Welsh saints are known for having established multiple monasteries during their lives, and early monasticism in Wales was largely eremitic rather than cenobitic. Welsh monastics imitated the pattern established by St. Anthony the Great in Egypt, which is why the early Welsh saints sometimes are called the Desert Fathers of Wales.[18] They were known for their extreme ascetic

---

18   J. B. Davies, 9.

practices, again modeled after the manner of the saints in Egypt,[19] but even more intense because they did not make allowances for the differences in climate between the dry deserts of Egypt and the cold, damp weather of Wales. However, the Welsh monastics did contrast with their Egyptian counterparts in one respect: Though both groups lived largely in eremitic communities comprised of individual cells, gathering together as a community for the Sunday Liturgy and feast days, the Welsh "hermits" typically did not remain permanently cloistered in their cells as did many of the Desert Fathers. Instead, they used their cells as what we might call "home bases." They were places of refuge and prayer, but otherwise the saints would spend time traveling about in missionary activity, converting pagans, establishing churches and monasteries, and building up the faithful.[20] The cenobitic model (living within communities collectively in one large building, such as we tend to think of monasteries today) did not take hold in Wales until Norman times and existed only in a small number of cases—usually for women's monasteries—after St. Gwenfrewy introduced it in the seventh century.[21]

Holy Wells

Many of the saints in this book are associated with holy wells in Wales. Holy wells (a well is actually a natural spring, *ffynnon* in Welsh) long have been a tradition in Orthodox countries from Greece to Russia, and they are an especially common phenomenon throughout the British Isles. It is believed that more than a thousand have been catalogued in these isles over the centuries. Hundreds have been known in Wales itself, many of which still exist, though they rarely are

---

19 Gerald Morgan, 58.
20 Jones et al., 66 and 82–85; and Oliver Davies, *Celtic Christianity*, 9–11 and 67.
21 Anonymous, "Saint Winifred and Her Holy Spring."

associated today with any kind of spiritual properties. Just as modern society favors rejecting accounts of miraculous events in saints' lives, it likewise tends to dismiss any account of a miraculous origin or working of any of these wells. As Orthodox believers, we do not so easily dismiss all such accounts, though it must be acknowledged that many stories regarding holy wells in particular are likely later embellishments from the late medieval period; a number of accounts border on magic or sorcery—sometimes even of a sinister nature—that, if true, would be clearly demonic rather than holy.

Wells have been viewed as special places in the British Isles since pre-Christian times. The pagan Celts often associated spiritual significance with natural springs, particularly those that provided healing benefits because of their high mineral content. Since water is one of life's foremost necessities, it is no wonder that the ancient Celts viewed any source of clean, pure water bursting from the ground as something enchanted or miraculous. They believed that elemental spirits inhabited and controlled these waters, and they would throw votive offerings into them—the origin of today's custom of tossing coins into fountains or "wishing wells."

As Christianity took root among the Celts, the spiritual aspect of these water sources remained strong but, as with other pre-Christian societal activities, they were "baptized" and made to have meaning within a Christian context. Just as when Pope Gregory in 601 instructed St. Augustine not to destroy pagan temples in Britain but to convert them into Christian churches so that the people would continue to frequent the places they already associated with worship, so these pagan "holy wells" were not filled in but were themselves converted to redirect the people's devotion to Christ and away from pagan deities. Already places of pilgrimage, the wells retained this spiritual significance so that Christian believers would come to them in devotion now to Christ and His saints rather than to naiads or other water sprites.

Not all holy wells are of pagan origin, however, and there are a number that sprang forth through a Christian saint's intercession when a need for water existed (as with Moses in the Old Testament), or in some cases arising at a place where a saint was martyred. A great number of these wells had churches built next to them, hence the reason so many older churches in Wales bear the names of early saints.

Earliest Welsh Saints

FIRST CENTURY

St. Cyllin

Saint Cyllin was born in Glamorgan around the year AD 50. The son of Caradoc ap Brân, King of Siluria and Eurgain, he was the last pendragon[22] of Britain. It is believed that his brother Linus was the friend of St. Paul in Rome mentioned in 2 Timothy 4:21. As such, Cyllin was familiar with Christian teaching through his family, and he traveled to Rome to be baptized (possibly by St. Paul himself), thus becoming the first Christian king in Britain.

Cyllin was considered a very wise and just king who ruled his people well. Many of his subjects embraced the Christian Faith through the teachings of other godly men from Greece and Rome whom Cyllin invited to Wales. He is said to have been the first of the Welsh kings to give infants names. Previously, children had been known only by something characteristic to their looks or manners; proper names were only for adults.[23]

Saint Cyllin had at least three sons and two daughters. He died while in Rome at a great old age around the year 150 and was buried there.

Though recognized as a pre-congregational[24] and pre-Schism saint, St. Cyllin has no known feast day on the church calendar.

---

22   A Briton war chief.
23   Richard Morgan, *St. Paul in Britain,* 161.
24   A pre-congregational saint is one who was declared to be a saint prior to the establishment of the Congregation for the Causes of Saints by the Roman Catholic Church.

St. Eigen

A sister of St. Cyllin, St. Eigen was the first female Christian saint among the Britons. She is believed to have traveled to Rome with St. Cyllin, where the two were baptized into the Faith, and on their return they formed a religious school called Cor Eurgain to introduce Christianity to the island. It likely was to this institution that St. Cyllin invited Christians from Greece and Rome to come and instruct the people, and it was through this "Choir of Eurgain" that many Welsh people embraced the holy Faith.

It is not known when St. Eigen reposed, nor is there a known feast day for her on the church calendar.

Alternate spellings: Eurgain, Eurgan, Eurgen

St. Ilid

Exactly who St. Ilid was is unknown, but many believe that he was Joseph of Arimathea since he was referred to as a "man of Israel"[25] and was a Jewish convert to Christianity. He came to Wales from Rome with Ss. Cyllin and Eigen and helped them establish the college of Cor Eurgain and thus played a major role in converting the land to Christ.

Nothing further is known of St. Ilid. He is commemorated on June 30.

---

25   Griffin, *Glastonbury and the Grail*, 96–97.

SECOND CENTURY

Ss. Deruvian and Ffagan

Almost nothing is known about the lives of these two early saints. They are said to have been sent to Wales by Pope Eleutherius around the year 180 in response to a letter from King Lucius of Britain requesting baptism into the Christian Faith. Because of their mission, they are sometimes referred to as the apostles of Britain. Evidence seems to point to their missionary activity primarily in southern Wales.

Saints Deruvian and Ffagan are both commemorated on May 26.

Alternate spellings: Deruvianus, Duvian, Dwywan, Dyfan / Fagan, Faganus, Fugatius, Pagan, Phagan, Phaganus

St. Tyfanog

All that is known of St. Tyfanog is that he arrived in Britain probably shortly after Ss. Deruvian and Ffagan. His principal work was on Ramsey Island off St. David's Head in Pembrokeshire, where he established a religious community. It is believed that he was martyred by the pagan natives of the island.

Saint Tyfanog is commemorated on November 25.

Alternate spellings: Dyfanog, Tauannauc

THIRD CENTURY

St. Amphibalus

Saint Amphibalus was a Christian priest in Rome. When Emperor Diocletian began his persecution of Christians, Amphibalus fled to Britain and came eventually to the Roman city of Verulamium (in modern-day Hertfordshire, England). There he was given shelter by a local pagan named Alban. Alban observed Amphibalus's extreme devotion to Christ and saw that despite the troubles of his life in exile, he remained at peace. Over time he asked Amphibalus to teach him more about Christ and the Church, and eventually Alban converted from his pagan ways and became a Christian himself (now recognized as St. Alban).

As Diocletian's persecutions continued, the Roman soldiers at Verulamium learned of Amphibalus and that he was hiding in Alban's home. When they came to arrest Amphibalus, Alban donned Amphibalus's clothes and surrendered himself as the man the soldiers were seeking. Alban was taken away and martyred, thus becoming one of the first British martyrs for Christ.

After Alban was executed, Amphibalus fled to Caerleon in Wales, where he converted many to Christ. Among his converts are believed to be Julius and Aaron, martyrs St. Gildas later mentioned in his history of Christianity in Britain. The Romans eventually captured Amphibalus and took him back to Verulamium, where he was martyred on June 25 in the year 304.

Saint Amphibalus is commemorated on June 25.

St. Caron

Almost nothing is known about St. Caron beyond his name and that he was associated with the area of Tregaron in Dyfed.[26] It is believed that he was a bishop of this region in the third century. Obviously a saint who made a notable impression on the Christians in his community, Christians at Tregaron have venerated him throughout the ages.

Saint Caron is commemorated on March 5.

---

26   Hutchison-Hall, *Orthodox Saints of the British Isles,* vol. 1, 161.

FOURTH CENTURY

St. Elen

Saint Elen was the wife of Magnus Maximus (known as Macsen Wledig in Welsh), the fourth-century emperor of Britain, Gaul, and Spain. Because her name in English is Helen, she is often confused with Helen of Constantinople. This confusion is made more acute by the fact that both Helens were wives of emperors and both had sons named Constantine (Cystennin in Welsh). For that reason, Elen is typically referred to today in English as St. Helen of Caernarfon and in Welsh as St. Elen Luyddog.

Very little is known about Elen's life, though she is credited with having introduced the Celtic form of monasticism to Wales after she and her husband met with St. Martin of Tours while visiting Gaul. There seems little doubt that she led an exemplary Christian life, as two of her five sons also became saints (St. Cystennin and St. Peblig), both of whom aided their mother in establishing monasteries.

Before Magnus Maximus was killed in battle in 388, Elen apparently influenced him to build roads across Wales so that soldiers could more easily be transported to defend the land against invaders. Hence her moniker Elen Luyddog, which means "Elen of the Hosts."[27]

There is a holy well bearing the name of St. Helen (Elen) in Caernarfon, Gwynedd,[28] that in centuries past was a site of pilgrimage for many who sought healing from its waters. Nothing remains today of any structures built around the well, though its waters can still be heard flowing underground.

Although Elen's exact dates of birth and death are not known, she lived in the fourth century. Saint Elen is commemorated on May 22.

Alternate spelling: Elin, Helen

St. Germanus (Garmon)

Although not Welsh by birth, this saint generally is listed with the saints from Wales because of his powerful influence in helping combat the heresy of Pelagianism that was vexing the church in Britain in the fourth century. He often is confused with another saint of the

---

27 Pennick, *The Celtic Saints*, 45.
28 See https://wellhopper.wales/2013/11/12/ffynnon-elen-dolwyddelan/ and https://thejournalofantiquities.com/2016/01/29/st-helens-holy-well -caernarfon-gwynedd-wales/.

fifth century who bears not only the same Welsh name (Garmon) but also the same feast day. The St. Garmon described below is known as St. Germanus of Auxerre.[29]

Born in Gaul around the middle to late fourth century, Germanus was of noble birth and was educated in Arles, Lyon, and Rome. He excelled in all his studies and became known at the imperial court for his eloquence and his knowledge of the law. He practiced law in Rome for several years, and later Emperor Flavius Honorius made him governor of some Roman provinces. As governor he took up residence in Auxerre in what is now central France. There, Germanus was tonsured a deacon by St. Amator (the bishop of Auxerre). This tonsure was completely against Germanus's will, but he nevertheless devoted himself wholeheartedly to his religious duties. When St. Amator died, Germanus was chosen unanimously to take his place, and he became well-known for his care of the poor and for his wise counsel in leading the Church.

Late in life, Germanus was called to Britain to help quell the influence of the Pelagian heresy that was threatening the church there. On his way to Britain, he passed through the region of Nanterre (near Paris) where he was greeted by a large crowd of people. Germanus singled out a young girl in the crowd and called her to himself and pronounced that she should live as one who is betrothed to Christ. The young maiden followed his admonition and later became known as St. Genevieve, the patron saint of Paris.

In Britain, Germanus debated with the bishops who had been taken in by the false teachings of Pelagius, and he confounded them with his acumen and eloquence. Once he had guided these erring bishops back to the truth, Germanus gave thanks at the shrine of St. Alban for their salvation. During that night St. Alban appeared to Germanus in a dream and revealed to him the details of his

---

29 Jones et al., *History of Christianity in Wales*, 32.

martyrdom. When he awoke Germanus had this revelation written out, and this became the principal source of the cult of St. Alban in Britain. During his time in Britain, Germanus also was asked to help the Britons defeat an army of Picts and Saxons who were attempting to invade their land. He placed himself at the head of the Britons and led the troops into a valley to confront the enemy. He had given them an order to shout "Alleluia!" at his signal, and when they did it so frightened the pagan invaders that they ran from the field, leaving their arms and baggage behind.

Saint Germanus returned to Auxerre after that and continued to work for his people. Around the year 440 he reposed in Ravenna, where he had traveled to petition the Roman government for mercy toward the citizens of Armorica.[30]

Saint Germanus is commemorated universally on July 31 but on August 3 in Wales.

Alternate spellings: Garmon, Germain

---

30 A region in Gaul that included Brittany and Normandy.

Golden Age of Saints

FIFTH CENTURY

St. Cadoc

Saint Cadoc was born around the year 497 in Monmouthshire, the eldest son of King Gwynllyw and Gwladys. Gwynllyw was a "robber chieftain" and a violent ruler who led frequent raids seemingly just for the thrill of it. That Cadoc would be born to such a father is itself somewhat miraculous, and indeed it is said that miracles occurred with Cadoc even before he was born. An angel foretold his birth, and while he was still in his mother's womb heavenly lights were reported to have appeared in his parents' house and the cellars remained miraculously stocked with food. When he was born, an angel directed the hermit Meuthi to come baptize him, and a holy well sprang up for his baptism.[31]

Despite these miraculous events, Cadoc's father was not soon to give up his turbulent ways and celebrated the child's birth by leading a number of his men on a wild raid through the countryside. Among the things they stole was the cow of an Irish monk named Tathyw (later St. Tathyw), the abbot of a nearby monastery. Tathyw was unafraid of Gwynllyw and his men and boldly went to the king, demanding the return of his cow. Impressed with the abbot's intrepid

---

31   The location of this holy well is unknown.

23

courage, the king decided to send young Cadoc to be educated at Tathyw's monastery. Cadoc advanced in his studies, both secular and sacred, and grew to cherish the monastic life. When he came of age, he chose not to lead his father's army but preferred becoming a warrior for Christ.

One day as he was traveling near Cardiff, the young monk began to be chased by an armed swineherd who belonged to an enemy tribe. As Cadoc ran through the forest looking for a place to hide, he accidentally came upon a wild boar, white with age. Startled by the monk, the boar charged Cadoc, who could see that he was in a hopeless situation. But as the boar lunged toward him, it suddenly disappeared. Cadoc saw this as a miraculous deliverance and marked the spot of his rescue with three tree branches. The Vale of Glamorgan where this took place was found to belong to Cadoc's uncle, King Pawl of Penychen, who after hearing of the miraculous event, gifted the valley to Cadoc. It was here that Cadoc later established the famous monastery, seminary, and hospital of Llancarfan.

The land seemed an unlikely place to establish such a collection of buildings, since it consisted mostly of a tangled marsh. But since Cadoc perceived that God had directed him to this place, he and his monks set about transforming the valley by draining the marsh and cultivating the land into one of the most well-known centers of religion in southern Wales.

Once the community was firmly established, Cadoc went to Ireland to study for three years, but on his return he found that the buildings had fallen into disrepair from neglect. Incensed at this, Cadoc immediately put his monks to work felling trees and rebuilding the structures that had been so sorely neglected during his absence. In the process, two wild stags came out of the forest and helped drag the heavy timbers, then went back to the forest when the work was done. Because of this miracle the stream running next to the monastery was called Nant Carfan (stag brook).

Many famous religious leaders were educated at Llancarfan under the tutelage of Cadoc, among them St. Illtud. Cadoc, who himself was noted for his great intellect and wisdom, also invited the renowned scholar St. Gildas to come teach at the seminary at Llancarfan, which he did for a year. During his stay he compiled a Gospel book that was kept in the monastery church and was beloved by the Welsh people.

In addition to being a place of learning, Llancarfan was known for its care of the poor. It became so renowned for its generosity that once when a band of robbers was approaching the monastery to raid it, they were met by St. Cadoc and his monks singing hymns to God. The robbers stopped suddenly and were so ashamed of their original intent that they turned and went away.

Cadoc's exemplary life of holiness led even his recalcitrant father to embrace the monastic life, and it is said that both he and his wife, Gwladys, became hermits and themselves were venerated as saints after their repose.

Eventually Cadoc grew too old to maintain his stewardship of the community and he withdrew to live at an unknown place (possibly the Isle of Flat Holm in the Bristol Channel). He is believed to have been martyred by pagan Saxons in Weedom while serving the Liturgy, sometime around the year 580.

Saint Cadoc is commemorated on September 25.

Alternate spellings: Cadocus, Cadog, Ca'ttwg

St. Garmon

Saint Garmon (not to be confused with fourth-century St. Germanus of Auxerre) was born around the year 410 in Brittany. He was cousin to St. Patrick of Ireland, and while still young went to Ireland where he studied with his cousin for several years. Settling later in Wales, he met St. Illtud, and he and Illtud together established the famous monastery of Llanilltud Fawr.

Garmon is said to have contested with King Gwrtheyrn (Vortigern) in a series of magical feats of strength on the Llŷn Peninsula[32] and to have established a number of churches throughout Wales. He is believed to have served as bishop on the Isle of Man later in life.

Saint Garmon died around the year 480 and is commemorated on July 31.

Alternate spellings: Garmonus, Germanus, Harmon

St. Illtud

We are fortunate in that an early reference to St. Illtud survives in the *Vita Sancti Samsonis,* a life of St. Samson, which was written less than one hundred years after Illtud's repose. From this we learn that Illtud, who had been a student of Germanus, was an illustrious scholar "in the knowledge of Scripture and in every branch of philosophy, poetry and rhetoric."[33] He also had been blessed with the gift of prophecy.

The exact date and place of St. Illtud's birth are uncertain, though it seems most credible to accept his date of birth around the year 475 and that he was born in Llydaw. According to a life written in 1140 (notably post-Schism and at least six centuries after his repose), his parents were of noble blood and had him educated for service in the Church. Illtud, however, was said to have chosen instead a military career and served as a knight in western Britain (now Wales).

A story tells that while on a hunting expedition with some fellow soldiers on land belonging to a local monastery, the group sent a message to the abbot (St. Cadoc) gruffly demanding that he prepare a meal for them. Although the demand was highly disrespectful, St. Cadoc graciously gave them a meal, recalling the instruction of our

---

32 Spencer, *Guide to the Saints of Wales,* 39.
33 J. B. Davies, *Saints of Wales,* 4.

Lord that whoever gives a cup of cold water will by no means lose his reward. However, before the soldiers could partake of the meal they had so rudely demanded, the ground opened up and swallowed the lot—except for Illtud—as punishment for their irreverence.

Finding himself alone but spared this harsh judgment, Illtud fell on his knees before St. Cadoc to beg forgiveness for his impiety. Saint Cadoc forgave him, but instructed him to abandon his worldly way of life and remember his religious upbringing. Thus inspired, he left the military and went with his wife to live beside the River Nadafan.[34] There an angel instructed him to strive for a more solitary life, and thus he became a hermit by the River Hodnant in South Glamorgan.

At some point thereafter he met St. Garmon, and the two founded a monastery called Llanilltud Fawr. Many well-known saints became Illtud's pupils at this monastery, among them Ss. David, Gildas, Padarn, Paul Aurelian, and Samson. These (and others) became missionaries throughout Wales, Cornwall, and Brittany. Illtud himself founded a number of churches, and many more were named in his honor as far away as Llanelltyd in Gwynedd.

Illtud also founded a monastery near what is today Llanrhidian, in a grove surrounded by plentiful fields that were quite productive and from which he fed the hungry. It was perhaps at this location where he introduced a new method of plowing to Wales. Though an otherwise ideal location, these lands suffered from frequent flooding from the sea. These encroachments caused Illtud great strife. Several times he built and rebuilt embankments to hold back the sea, but repeatedly the waves crashed through them to flood the fields and erode the foundations of the buildings, including the oratory. Though loathe to abandon the site, Illtud finally had all he could endure of the persistent flooding and decided to relocate. The night before he was to leave, an angel came to him and directed him

---

34   Spencer, 46.

instead to remain, giving him instructions on how to drive back the sea. The following morning he went to the sea and drove it back as the angel had taught him to do. The sea fled before him "as if it were a sensible animal"[35] and left the lands dry, just as the waters had parted for Moses in Egypt, leaving dry ground before him. Illtud then struck the shore with his staff, and from where he thrust his staff a spring welled up, flowing with pure water despite being so close to the sea. Saint Illtud's well[36] flows to this day and is located in what is now a private garden near the Church of St. Rhydian and St. Illtud.

Although the year of Illtud's repose is not known, the *Vita Sancti Samsonis* does record an event that took place shortly before his death that validates his prophetic gift. As he was on his deathbed, Illtud summoned two abbots, Isanus and Atoclius, to his side. When they arrived he told them to "be of good cheer, for your own departure shall in each case quickly follow mine, though not with equal happiness for you both. . . . Brother Isanus shall see my soul carried away under the appearance of an eagle having two golden wings, and he shall also see . . . another eagle, but flying heavily with a pair of leaden wings, the soul of that other brother [Atoclius]. And after forty days brother Isanus shall himself also happily come to Christ."[37] Illtud died peacefully at midnight while the brothers chanted hymns around his bed. Isanus did indeed witness Illtud's soul ascending to heaven, and he also later saw the soul of Atoclius carried away with difficulty but at last released through the prayers of the saints. Forty days after this, Isanus himself died happily, just as Illtud had foretold.

Saint Illtud is commemorated on November 6.

---

35   Rees, *Lives of the Cambro Saints*, 478.

36   See https://www.mysteriousbritain.co.uk/ancient-sites/st-illtyds-well
     -llanrhidian/.

37   Doble, *Lives of the Welsh Saints*, 89.

The Holy Tribe of St. Brychan Brycheiniog

Brychan Brycheiniog was a Welsh nobleman of the fifth century who epitomized Proverbs 22:6 ("Train up a child in the way he should go, / And when he is old he will not depart from it"). So many of his children and descendants became saints that they sometimes are referred to as one of the Holy Families of Britain.

Brychan was the son of Irish King Anlach and his wife Marchel. Marchel was heiress to the kingdom of Garthmadryn in Wales, but she had traveled as a young maiden to Ireland to find respite from a particularly harsh Welsh winter. There she met Anlach and agreed to marry him, but only on the condition that they would raise their children in her homeland. Thus, soon after Brychan was born the family returned to Garthmadryn. When Brychan was four years old, he was entrusted to St. Drichan to be educated in the holy Faith.

At one point when he was a young man, Brychan was sent to Powys to be a hostage. This was a common practice of the day between two rival kingdoms: The son of one of the kings would become a hostage to the other in order to help ensure peace between them. King Banadl of Powys had been victorious in a war against King Anlach, and in order to guarantee that Anlach would honor the peace treaty, Brychan became a hostage of Banadl. While at Banadl's court, Brychan fell in love with Banhadlwedd, the king's daughter. As it was not permissible for a hostage to consort with his captor's daughter, Brychan secretly seduced her, possibly by force. When it was obvious that Banhadlwedd was with child, Banadl sent Brychan back to Garthmadryn with his daughter, now Brychan's wife, where she bore him his first son, Cynog (later St. Cynog).

After his father died, Brychan assumed the throne of Garthmadryn, where he raised his kingdom to such high status that it came to be named after him (Brycheiniog). Having repented of his youthful passions and being remorseful for past sins, he devoted himself

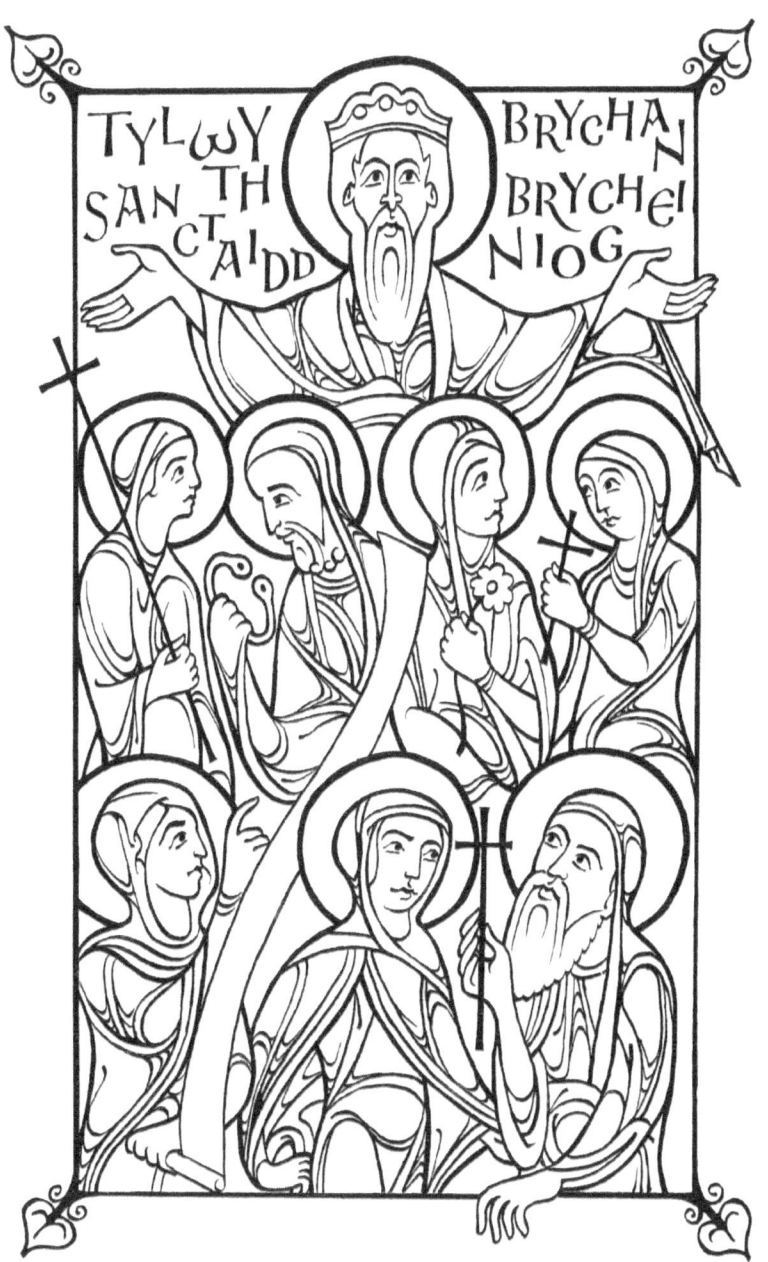

TYLWY TH SANCTAIDD BRYCHAN BRYCHEINIOG

solidly to following the way of Christ. He ruled wisely and was well known for his fair judgment and care of the poor. He also became a great benefactor of the Church. In his old age, Brychan is thought to have abdicated his throne to become a hermit.

Over the course of his reign he married three times, each wife blessing him with multiple children before dying. Tradition says that altogether he fathered twenty-four sons and as many daughters (some sources claim even more), many of whom became saints. Because he and his children were so well-known for their sanctity, it seems likely that at least some of those who were said to be his offspring actually were grandchildren or other relatives. In any case, these are among those of his children who became saints: *(sons)* Clether, Clydwyn, Cynog, Dingad, Dogfan, Dyfrig, and Nectan; *(daughters)* Adwen, Callwen, Cynheiddon, Dilic, Dwynwen, Eiliwedd, Gwen, Gwenfyl, Keyne, Llud, Mabyn, Menefrida, and Tydfil. While very little information survives about the lives of most of these holy children, seven appear in the following pages.

Saint Brychan is commemorated on April 6.

St. Cynheiddon (Endelienta)

One of the many children of St. Brychan Brycheiniog, St. Cynheiddon (often Latinized as Endelienta) was born probably around the year 470. Nothing of her youth is known, but it is clear that she was brought up in the Faith of Christ from childhood, since as a young maiden she crossed the Bristol Channel to join her siblings who were evangelizing Cornwall for Christ. On her way there, she apparently stopped on the Island of Lundy and converted its inhabitants, establishing a small chapel there (which later came to be dedicated erroneously to St. Helen).

Once she arrived in Cornwall, she stayed with her brother St. Nectan in Hartland for some time and later became a hermit at

Trentinney. Although she would return occasionally to exhort the Christians on Lundy, she chose a hermitic life and is said to have lived solely on cow's milk and water that she obtained from wells near her cell. Her sister, St. Dilic, also settled as a hermit at St. Illich not far from Cynheiddon, and the two often would visit each other and pray together. It was said that the grass on the path they trod was afterwards always greener than the surrounding turf.

One day Cynheiddon's cow strayed onto the land belonging to the Lord of Trentinney, and out of spite the lord killed it. When Cynheiddon's godfather learned of this outrage, he sent a contingent of soldiers to kill this lord, just as he had killed the innocent cow. Cynheiddon, however, was so despondent over learning of this revenge done in her name that she miraculously restored the lord to life.

Sometime after this St. Cynheiddon had a vision of her approaching death and, calling her friends together, she told them her last wishes. She said that once dead her body was to be placed on a cart yoked with two bullocks who then would be allowed to go wherever they willed. She was to be buried at the place they stopped.

On the 29th day of April sometime in the sixth century (the exact year is not known), St. Cynheiddon was martyred, either by Welsh pagans or by invading Saxons. Her friends did as she had requested, and the bullocks took her body to the top of a nearby hill. She was buried at that place, and a church (now known as St. Endellion) was built over her grave.

Saint Cynheiddon is commemorated on April 29.

Alternate spellings: Cenheidlon, Endelienta, Endellion

St. Cynog

The first of St. Brychan Brycheiniog's numerous offspring, Cynog was conceived when his father violated the daughter of King Banadl of Powys while he was being held hostage. Despite such an inauspicious beginning, Cynog grew up in one of the most devout Christian households in all of Wales.

As Cynog was his firstborn, Brychan presented his infant son with an ornate torc at his baptism. Brychan had worn this torc around his arm, but the infant Cynog wore it on his head. It would become a very famous relic in the history of Wales.

Little is known about Cynog's youth beyond the fact that from his earliest years he was instructed in the Faith and embraced it wholly. While still young he left his father's court to become a hermit near Y Gaer, where he devoted himself to prayer and to ministering to the people of Brycheiniog. Like many other hermits of his day, he also was a traveling missionary and at one point ventured across the Bristol Channel to join several of his siblings who were evangelizing Cornwall.

Returning later to Wales, he settled in Caer Wedros in Ceredigion, where he performed one of his most notable miracles. It seems that near Caer Wedros a tribe of pagan cannibals called *ormests* lived and were tormenting the local populace by attacking them at night. A young widow, recognizing Cynog's holiness, approached him and asked that he save her and her children from these ormests. Cynog agreed to stand guard at her door, praying all night for their deliverance. When the ormests arrived, Cynog offered to give their chief a slice of his own flesh from his thigh if in return they would spare the widow and her children. The ormest chief agreed, but the following night the ormests came again anyway to steal the widow and her children. Cynog defended the household by striking the chief ormest on the head with his torc. And just as David slew Goliath with only a small stone, so Cynog killed the ormest with a single blow from his torc. When the other ormests saw their chief lying dead, they fled in terror and were never seen again. Where Cynog had cut away the flesh from his thigh, something resembling snow-white wool grew over it to protect the wound.

News of Cynog's miraculous defeat of the ormests spread, but some scoffed at the idea that he could have slain their chief with a small torc. It is said that as Cynog passed one day by a blacksmith's, the smith mocked him regarding the legendary victory. To demonstrate the ridiculousness of such a story, the smith grabbed the torc, placed it on his anvil, and intended to demolish it with his hammer. When he struck the torc, however, only a few small splinters flew off it, piercing his eyes and causing him to live in darkness the rest of his life.[38]

Later in life Cynog joined a monastic community of hermits on a mountain known as Y Fan. The monks inhabited individual cells throughout this steep, rocky mountain, and Cynog built his cell near its very summit. There were no wells on the mountain, and so it was necessary for the monks to make a long trek to the river in order to collect water, which they then had to carry back up the steep hill. Most of the monks grumbled about this inconvenience, but Cynog— who would make this necessary journey cheerfully and with thanksgiving to God despite his advancing age—chastised them for their slothfulness and ingratitude.

The other monks came to resent Cynog as he clearly outshone them in holiness and perseverance. God soon blessed Cynog by having a small stream of water appear miraculously above his cell so that he would no longer have to make the tortuous journey each day to the river and back. This caused the envious monks to become even more hostile toward their brother, and they conspired to do away with Cynog so that they could acquire water from his spring. Thus, one morning they went to his cell and found him standing in prayer in the midst of the stream. In anger and bitter cupidity, they murdered the blessed saint by cutting off his head. As his head fell into

---

38 In other versions the splinter from the torc pierced the blacksmith's brain, killing him instantly.

the water, the spring immediately dried up and never flowed again. One of the monks took the torc that Cynog kept underneath his habit, and they buried his body where later the parish church of Merthyr Cynog was built.

Saint Cynog's torc became such a revered relic that throughout the region of Brycheiniog no one dared swear falsely in its presence. Like most relics from the distant past in Wales, the torc has since disappeared.

Saint Cynog is commemorated on October 7.

Alternate spellings: Canog, Kennauch

St. Dwynwen

Saint Dwynwen was a daughter of St. Brychan Brycheiniog, and of his several daughters, Dwynwen was said to be the most beautiful of all. One of the most beloved saints of Wales, Dwynwen nonetheless remains in many ways an enigma. There are multiple versions of her life, some even from modern times, but all of them center around themes of love and devotion. In recent decades St. Dwynwen has become prominent in popular culture throughout Wales, being adopted (and in many ways secularized) the way St. Valentine has been in most of the West—a kind of patron saint of love and romance. Most spiritual aspects of her life have been diminished in modern renditions of her story, and medieval legends have been interwoven with contemporary secular variations to make her almost a fairy-tale-like figure. The events presented below we might consider the most likely to be authentic when reviewing her life in context with her faith and by comparing all versions together.

From her youth Dwynwen longed for the ascetic life. As she neared adulthood, however, she became the object of affection of one Maelon Daffodrill, who fell madly in love with her. It seems that perhaps she also developed an attraction for Maelon and became conflicted about whether to pursue an ascetic or married life. Once she resolved to abandon the world in seclusion and virginity, she informed Maelon that she could not marry him, as she was devoting her life entirely to Christ.

This decision did not please Maelon, and his lustful passions made him desire her all the more. Having been denied her hand in marriage, Maelon attempted to take her by force. Dwynwen escaped from his hand but was brokenhearted. She loved Maelon, but she loved Christ more and had hoped that Maelon would understand her decision to devote herself to spiritual pursuits. Instead, he had revealed a dark and rapacious corner of his heart.

One night an angel appeared to Dwynwen in a dream and offered her a potion to drink. As if being healed from a disease, Dwynwen found the potion to have cured her from any passions remaining for marital joy with Maelon. But as a result of Maelon's evil bid to force himself upon her, he himself was turned to ice.

After learning of what had happened to Maelon, Dwynwen prayed earnestly to God that Maelon's sin would not be held against him and that he be restored to life. She further asked that all who sought to be bound together in true Christian marriage would succeed in their quest or, if that was not God's will, that they be freed from their passions and from their desire to be wed, just as she had been. As a result of her sincere prayers, Maelon indeed was delivered from ice, and Dwynwen never again was burdened with a yearning to marry but was free to pursue a life of ascetic devotion. She became a nun and spent the rest of her life in wholehearted service to Christ and to her fellow humans.

Some versions of her life say that following these events Dwynwen left her father's kingdom and traveled throughout Wales with her sister St. Keyne and brother St. Dyfnan, and that together they established a number of churches. In any case, she eventually settled on a small island near Anglesey known as Ynys Llanddwyn. Here she spent her days in unceasing prayer and care of those who came to her for aid. She studied the healing properties of local herbs and was able to help treat many bodily illnesses, but she also freely counseled and prayed for those suffering from sickness of the heart. During the sixty years Dwynwen dwelt on the island, people from all over Wales came to her for assistance and prayers.

Dwynwen reposed in the Lord at an unknown date and is believed to be buried near her church on Ynys Llanddwyn. The church at one time was one of the most frequented pilgrimage sites in Wales, rivaled only by St. Davids and St. Winifred's well in Holywell. Numerous cases of healings were reported at her well throughout the ages. After Henry VIII's Reformation, however, pilgrimages were outlawed and the site fell to ruin.

Though known today as the patron saint of love and marriage, Dwynwen is also the patron of sick animals. She is commemorated on January 25, which in Wales has become a largely secular celebration. Curiously, Dwynwen is venerated in the Orthodox Church but not (officially) in either the Roman Catholic or Anglican churches.

Alternate spellings: Donwen, Donwenna, Dwynwen

St. Eiliwedd

Like many other saints from the sub-Roman period,[39] very little is known of the life of St. Eiliwedd. One of several daughters of the righteous King St. Brychan Brycheiniog and sister of St. Dwynwen, she came from a very devout Christian family, as we have seen. That she died a virgin seems to indicate that she, like Dwynwen, chose a celibate life despite being, also like her sister, quite beautiful. Her beauty captured the heart of an invading Saxon prince who tried

---

39   The time between the end of Roman rule in Britain and the ascendency of the Anglo-Saxons.

to convince her to renounce Christ and marry him, a pagan. When she refused and attempted to flee from him, he chased her down and beheaded her at Slwch Tump. Where her head came to rest against a stone, a holy well sprang forth.[40] Many miraculous cures were reported to have occurred at this well before it was destroyed during the Reformation.

The virgin-martyr St. Eiliwedd is commemorated on August 1.

Alternate spellings: Almedha, Eled, Elevatha, Ellyw, Eluned, Llud

St. Keyne

Saint Keyne was one of the many daughters of the righteous King St. Brychan of Brycheiniog. Like St. Dwynwen she was of exceptional beauty and received many proposals of marriage in her youth, but having taken a vow of virginity she instead devoted her life entirely to Christ. Along with her brother St. Dyfnan and sister St. Dwynwen she traveled widely, founding churches in Glamorgan, Dyfed, and Gwent. After St. Dwynwen settled on Ynys Llanddwyn, Keyne withdrew to Cornwall and lived as a hermit for a number of years. She built her cell in what is now the village of St. Keyne.

Eventually Keyne's nephew, St. Cadoc, persuaded her to return to Wales. Perhaps it was on her return journey that she passed by what is now Keynsham, Somerset, where there was an area on the banks of the Avon that was uninhabitable because of the number of snakes that swarmed the grounds. Saint Keyne's prayers turned the snakes to stone, and the area became suitable for habitation.

Completing her journey to Wales, the saint finally settled in Powys beside a hill known today as Llangenny. Again, by the power of her prayers a healing spring burst forth from the ground, and she later

---

40 See https://en.wikipedia.org/wiki/Slwch_Tump.

built a chapel next to the holy well. The well remains to this day,[41] but the chapel was torn down in 1790.

Saint Keyne had many miracles associated with her, and she had the gift of prophecy. It is said that once when St. Cadoc was visiting her in Llangenny, she prophesied that her dwelling place would one day fall into the hands of sinful people but that others later would root them out and, by her prayers, find her tomb. At that time, she foretold, "the Lord's name would be blessed forever."[42]

Saint Keyne is believed to have reposed in the Lord sometime around the year 500 either in Llangenny or perhaps at Llangeinor, where another holy well with healing properties supposedly was located. To this day her tomb has not been discovered.

Saint Keyne is commemorated on October 8.

Alternate spellings: Cain, Cenau, Ceinwen, Cenedlon, Kayane, Keane, Keyna

St. Morwenna

Saint Morwenna was another of the many children of the righteous King St. Brychan Brycheiniog who became saints. Like her sisters Dwynwen and Keyne, Morwenna took monastic vows and remained a virgin. She studied in Ireland before going to Cornwall, where she made a hermitage at a place called Hennacliff, now known as Morwenstow. At Hennacliff she helped build a church with her own hands, often carrying large stones on her head. Once when she stopped to rest, she placed the stone on the ground and a holy well sprang up at that spot.[43]

---

41   See https://www.celticglory.com/spiritual/st-keynes-holy-well-st-keyne-cornwall.

42   Spencer, 52.

43   See https://www.megalithic.co.uk/article.php?sid=8175.

Shortly before Morwenna died, St. Nectan came to care for her, and one of her dying wishes was for him to raise her up so that she could see her native Welsh shore one last time. Although venerated as a Cornish saint, it is clear that she never forgot the country or the people of her birth. Morwenna is believed to have reposed in the early sixth century at her hermitage and to have been buried at Hennacliff.

Saint Morwenna is commemorated on July 8.[44]

Alternate spellings: Moorina, Mwynenna

St. Nectan

Saint Nectan was one of the many sons of the righteous King St. Brychan Brycheiniog. From his youth Nectan chose to renounce the world and become a slave of Christ. Inspired by the life of St. Anthony the Great, he yearned to imitate the struggles of the great Egyptian anchorite.

When St. Nectan was a young man, he left with a few companions to embark on missionary work to convert the pagans to Christ. Together they boarded a small boat with the intention of allowing God to take the helm. They vowed that wherever the boat stopped, there they would evangelize the people. The boat came to rest on the northwest coast of Devon near what is today the village of Hartland. The group settled in a dense forest near Stoke, and there St. Nectan built a cell, where he lived in fervent prayer and strict asceticism. It is said that he would spend most of his time in solitude, seeing his family only once a year during the Nativity, when they would visit him in order to pray together.

---

44   Saint Morwenna is not to be confused with St. Modwenna, who is commemorated on July 5.

One of the validations of an anchorite's holiness is the fact that despite spending much of their lives in deep isolation, often far-removed from civilization, people nonetheless would come to know about them and seek them out for guidance. Such was the case with St. Nectan. One day in the year 510, a local swineherd named Huddon came to beseech his help in finding some missing sows. The saint was able to direct him to the sows, and in gratitude Huddon gave St. Nectan two milk cows.

On June 17 of that year, two robbers wandered past St. Nectan's hermitage and, seeing his cows, stole them for themselves. When Nectan realized the cows were missing, he tracked them through the forest and came upon the thieves. He spoke with them and encouraged them to abandon their pagan ways and accept Christ. Instead, they killed St. Nectan, and one of the thieves cut off his head. The saint then took up his head, walked to his holy well,[45] set his head upon a rock, and lay down and expired. At such a sight the thief who had decapitated Nectan went mad. The other thief immediately repented of his deed, accepted the Faith, and reverently buried the martyred saint.

That St. Nectan still prays for us is evident in an event that occurred more than 400 years after his death. On the eve of the Battle of Brunanburh (937), King Æthelstan's army was preparing for battle against three other kings. Victory did not look favorable, especially since a plague had been decimating his troops. That night one of Æthelstan's soldiers could tell that he too was falling victim to the plague, and he began pleading to God and St. Nectan to deliver him. His cries were loud enough that King Æthelstan heard him in an adjacent tent, though he was not familiar with this saint. Around midnight St. Nectan appeared to the young soldier, touched the afflicted part of

---

45   See https://insearchofholywellsandhealingsprings.wordpress.com/2015/06
      /19/the-wells-of-st-nectan-hartland-devonshire/.

his body, and the man was healed immediately. The next morning the soldier stood before King Æthelstan and related all that had happened, and he told the king that he should pray to St. Nectan for success in the day's battle. Though King Æthelstan had not known the saint before, he did as he had been bidden, and he won the battle. The plague also miraculously passed, and from that day the king held St. Nectan in very high esteem and helped support his church.[46]

The holy martyr St. Nectan is commemorated on June 17.

Alternate spelling: Nighton

---

46   Lapa, "Holy Martyr Nectan of Hartland."

SIXTH CENTURY

St. Asaph

No biography of St. Asaph survives, so what little we know about him today is from references to him in the *Life of St. Kentigern,* written by Jocelyn of Furness around 1185. Saint Kentigern (518–614) was a Scottish saint who brought Christianity to Glasgow and labored there for many years. Around 545 the pagan King Morken drove out this holy man, and Kentigern found refuge in Wales. There he founded a monastery at Llanelwy, which drew nearly 1,000 disciples, among them a young Asaph.

An early miracle of St. Asaph revealed the special calling of this humble monk to St. Kentigern. Saint Kentigern had a practice of standing in the icy river water to pray, often for long periods at a time, and once when he emerged from the water, suffering bitterly from the cold, he asked the young Asaph to fetch him some wood with which to build a fire. Instead, Asaph returned carrying live coals in his cloak without any ill effect. This revealed to Kentigern the sanctity of the young monk, and Asaph became his dearest disciple. Saint Kentigern later ordained him to the priesthood.

When the anti-Christian King Morken died, he was succeeded by a more tolerant monarch who invited Kentigern to return to Scotland. When he did, St. Asaph was consecrated bishop to succeed Kentigern and thus was the first Welsh bishop of his diocese.

Saint Asaph is believed to have died around the year 596 and was buried in his cathedral. He is commemorated on May 1 in the Orthodox Church.

Alternate spellings: Asaf, Asa, Asáphi

St. Brynach

Saint Brynach is believed to have been born in Ireland around the year 500. His parents were of noble rank in their pagan society, but Brynach converted to Christianity probably while in his late teens. After his conversion he made a pilgrimage to Rome, where legend has it he confronted a fearsome beast that had been terrorizing the local populace. After praying for strength as David did before Goliath, Brynach threw the dreadful creature to the ground and killed it.

After this pilgrimage Brynach made his way first to Brittany, where he performed many miracles of healing, and then on to what is now Milford Haven in Pembrokeshire, Wales. There he was pursued by a local nobleman's daughter, who tried to entice him to immoral acts, but he resisted all her advances. She even mixed a cup of wolfsbane as a love potion and presented it to him while wearing alluring attire, but this too he refused. Unused to being rebuffed, the damsel became enraged and her love turned into hatred for Brynach. She enlisted the help of a band of miscreants to persecute him so that he might give in to her wishes, but failing that, they were not to let him go away alive. When Brynach did not heed their injunction to accept the damsel's advances, one of the men pierced him with a spear and the others rushed to complete the murder. Brynach was rescued from their clutches, however, and the judgment of God came quickly upon the man who had speared the saint. He was set upon by a host of winged lice, which tortured him for the rest of his days and led him eventually to a miserable death.

Severely injured from the spear, Brynach went to a nearby well,[47] washed away the blood from the wound, and was healed. The well was known thereafter as Fons Rubens (Red Well), and God bestowed many healings through its waters.

Brynach and his companions later came to Nevern and chose it as a suitable place to build a monastery. For three days they labored at felling trees and hewing lumber. But when they rose from sleep on the fourth day, they found nothing remaining to show for all their labors—not a single log or plank could be found. It was as if the ground had swallowed up everything they had made. Brynach took this as a work of Almighty God and instructed his fellows to fast and pray so that they might be shown the meaning of it all.

The following night as Brynach was engaged in prayer an angel appeared to him and told him that this was not to be the place of his dwelling. Instead, he was told to follow the bank of the river to the second rill and watch until he should see a wild white sow with piglets. At that place, the angel said, he was to build his dwelling. When the saint proceeded down the river the next day, he saw exactly what had been foretold, and there he and his companions built a fire and spent the whole of the night in prayer and thanksgiving.

As it happened, this land belonged to a certain lord named Clether who was a devout Christian and well advanced in years. When he saw the smoke from Brynach's fire the next morning, he called together his twenty sons and told them that the man whom God had long ago promised to send to them had arrived. They then went as one to St. Brynach, fell down before him in gratitude for the providence of God, and yielded themselves completely to Brynach's spiritual direction. These twenty sons of Lord Clether all became monks under St. Brynach and remained with him. Lord Clether himself withdrew to Cornwall and faithfully served God there until the end of his earthly life.

---

47   See https://www.megalithic.co.uk/article.php?sid=24590.

Saint Brynach was known for his sincere devotion with continual fasting, frequent vigils, and bodily discipline, training himself by bathing in cold water daily. Whatever goods he and his companions could produce, he converted to the use of the poor. His life so pleased our Lord that he frequently enjoyed the visitation of holy angels with which he would discourse when they met on the top of a hillock called Carningli (Mountain of Angels).[48]

God magnified the saint such that he could tame wild beasts whenever they could be of service. It is said that when he wished to move heavy objects he would call two wild stags from a herd, have them draw the cart the desired distance, then release them to return to the wild once again. Brynach also had a cow that he kept separate from the rest because of its unusual size and because it could produce such an abundance of milk. This cow he put under the care of a tamed wolf, which would lead it to pasture in the morning and return it home in the evening.

It happened one day that King Maelgwn of Cambria journeyed with his men through the area and encamped for the night near Brynach's cell. He sent orders for Brynach to prepare supper for him and his companions. Though Brynach always freely fed the poor, he felt no compunction whatever to yield to the unjust commands of this belligerent monarch. The king, being an irascible sort, took great umbrage at this and sent his men to take Brynach's cow and butcher it for supper. He also said that the next day he would banish Brynach and his companions from his kingdom and burn down all their buildings. When Brynach learned what had happened to his beloved cow, he simply laid his complaint before God and committed the whole case to His divine will.

---

48   See https://en.wikipedia.org/wiki/Mynydd_Carningli.

The king's servants who had seized the cow cut it into pieces and prepared it for cooking. But although they had built a fire beneath the cauldron, the water in it refused to boil and remained cold. They threw more wood on the fire, but this had no effect on the water. The king then perceived that this was by the will of God in retribution for his prideful and selfish acts of stealing and butchering Brynach's cow. Great fear then came upon him and his men, and they went in humility with bare feet to fall down before Brynach and beg for his forgiveness. They confessed to having sinned by stealing and killing the cow and vowed never to do such things again. Brynach harbored no bitterness toward the king and prayed to God on his behalf. He then, in the presence of all, restored the cow to life and out of compassion bade the king and his men to spend the night with them.

Knowing that his guests were still hungry, he had them sit at table while he picked bread from a nearby oak, drew wine from the River Caman, and gathered fish in great abundance from the same source. With these miraculous gifts, the king and all his retinue were satisfied beyond their expectations, and they slept peacefully throughout the night.

The following morning the king returned Brynach's beneficence by exempting him from royal taxations that would otherwise have applied to his monastery, dwellings, and all the lands thereabout. Brynach accepted the king's gift, blessed him, and gave thanks to God for such favor.

Brynach pleased God all his life, and God performed many other miracles through him over the course of his time on earth. The Lord received him into His own Kingdom on the seventh day of April (or January according to some sources) around the year 570, and his relics were buried below the eastern wall of his church in Nevern.

Saint Brynach is commemorated on April 7.

Alternate spellings: Brenach, Bernachius

St. Cadfan

No authentic life of St. Cadfan survives, so most of what we know of his deeds is from a twelfth-century *awdl*[49] by Llywelen the Bard. This source, however, does not give us information about Cadfan's dates, but it is believed he was born circa 440 in Brittany, the son of Eneas Lydewig and Gwen Teirbron, and grandson of Budic II of Brittany. About his youth we know little, but given the character of his life we may assume that he was brought up in the Faith and was most eager to share the love of Christ with all. He is believed to have erected churches in Brittany even while he was still young, before crossing the sea to Wales.

Around the year 465, Cadfan left Brittany with a large group of monks, intent on missionary work in Wales. It is known that shortly after arriving he founded a church in Tywyn on land granted to him by King Cyngar, and he later established a church in Llangadfan. He built a *clas*[50] in Tywyn, which is believed to have been the first in Wales, and he was one of the chief founders of monasticism in that part of the country.

In 516 he moved to Bardsey Island (Ynys Enlli) and founded a monastery that became one of the most illustrious in all of Wales. Prince Einion Frenin of Lleyn appointed him abbot, and he oversaw the monastery for the next twenty-six years. During this time he made a number of missionary journeys throughout Wales, establishing churches and monasteries.

When the pagan Saxons began invading the British Isles around 610, they destroyed the monastery at Bangor Fawr and attacked many others, forcing monks from all across Britain to flee. Many came to

---

49 An *awdl* is a Welsh form of poetry in strict meter.
50 A *clas* was a large church that housed an entire religious community, as opposed to later monasteries that consisted of a large building surrounded by smaller supporting buildings (kitchens, cloisters, etc.).

Bardsey, and the island's population grew exponentially so that over a period of time as many as twenty thousand monks lived at the monastery. The island soon became known as the "Iona of Wales,"[51] and the sanctity of the place was so renowned that in later years three pilgrimages to Bardsey were considered equal to a pilgrimage to Rome, making it equal in status to St. Davids in that regard.

Neither the year nor the place of Cadfan's repose are known for certain, though he is believed to have died around 542. Sadly, nothing remains of the great monastery on Bardsey Island, though the church of Tywyn survives to this day. A holy well[52] nearby was for many centuries a place of pilgrimage, and its waters were known especially for curing rheumatism, scrofula, and skin diseases. The well may be visited today.

Saint Cadfan is commemorated on November 1.

Alternate spellings: Cadvan, Canu, Catamanus, Gadfan, Gabriel

---

51 Lapa, "Venerable Cadfan of Bardsey."
52 See https://coflein.gov.uk/en/site/32397/.

St. Cenydd

So little of Cenydd's life is reliably documented that some people believe he is merely a legend. But the number of ancient churches in Wales and Brittany that were named in his honor, and the fact that his name appears in early liturgical calendars, give credence to his existence.

What we know of his life appears in later medieval anchorite traditions. According to those sources, Cenydd was the son of King Deroch II of Domnonee, the product of an incestuous relationship the king had with his own daughter. Cenydd was born with a deformity of the legs, the calf of one leg attached to the thigh. A priest baptized the newborn, christening him Cenydd, before Deroch mercilessly ordered that this defective child be thrown into the river. Someone with more mercy than his father made a cradle for the poor child out of osiers. Cenydd was laid inside, and the crib was placed in the River Lliw. The river's current carried the cradle out to sea, where a storm threw it onto the shore of Ynys Weryn. Here Cenydd was cared for miraculously by a group of seagulls, and after nine days an angel descended to care for and instruct the boy in the Christian Faith. During this time the clothes in which he had been discarded grew with him as bark does on a tree.

When Cenydd was eighteen years old, the angel who had been attending him told him that he should leave the place and go to a reedy spot about a mile distant. Once he arrived there, after great effort because of his crippled leg, Cenydd built himself a hut of osiers and acquired a servant. Here, along with his servant (who likely was a disciple), he became a hermit and devoted himself to prayer. Later a church was built on this spot known as Llangennydd.

One day a band of robbers came upon Cenydd's cell, but he greeted them with hospitality, which they accepted. They left their weapons outside the hut and later found one of their spears missing. Cenydd's servant swore that he had not seen it, but in reality he had coveted the spear and stolen it for himself. Having lied under oath, the servant went mad and, like Nebuchadnezzar of old, lived as a wild beast in the forest. Cenydd prayed for his restoration, and after seven years the servant repented and returned to Cenydd's service in deep contrition.

In 545 the Council of Llanddewi Brefi was called, and St. David traveled about the Welsh countryside summoning area bishops and abbots to the synod. He passed by Cenydd's cell, where he was treated hospitably. Impressed by Cenydd's holiness and wisdom, St. David invited Cenydd to come with him to the council, but Cenydd declined because of his crippled leg. Saint David then prayed for healing, and God made Cenydd's leg whole. Cenydd, however, was not pleased by this and, feeling unworthy, asked to be restored to the way God originally had made him. Thus St. David prayed again and Cenydd's calf once more went up and adhered itself to the thigh. As a result Cenydd did not in fact attend the council, but word of him spread and soon, enough disciples came to see him that a monastery was established at Llangennydd.

Saint Cenydd is commemorated on August 1, as he reposed on that date sometime around 587. (In Llangennydd his feast day is celebrated on July 5.)

Alternate spellings: Cennydd, Kenneth, Kined, Kyned, Kynedus

St. Clydog

A grandson of St. Brychan Brycheiniog, Clydog's father was St. Clydwyn.[53] He studied for the priesthood under St. Cadoc at Llancarfan but was called instead to assume the throne of Ergyng when his father died. There he ruled with great wisdom and justice, issuing in a time of peace and prosperity for his kingdom.

At one point the daughter of a nobleman of Ergyng fell madly in love with King Clydog and said she would never marry anyone else. A Saxon noble in Clydog's court developed an interest in the same woman, but she refused his advances, stating that she was devoted in love to Clydog. When the king was out hunting one day with the Saxon noble, the Saxon in jealousy shot him with an arrow. The hunting party put the king on an oxcart, which was driven to a ford in the river. At that point the cart broke down and the oxen could not be driven any further. There the king died, and he was buried on that spot.

The people of Ergyng greatly mourned the loss of their wise and beloved king and built a chapel over his grave at Clodock (Merthir Clitauc), now in Herefordshire, England.[54]

Saint Clydog is commemorated on November 3.

Alternate spellings: Cladocus, Cleodicus, Clodock, Clydawg

---

53   Some sources claim that Clydwyn, not Cynog, was the eldest son of Brychan Brycheigniog, but there is insufficient evidence to support this.

54   See https://www.wilcuma.org.uk/a-century-of-english-sanctity/29-saint-clydog/.

St. Cybi

Although born in Cornwall, St. Cybi was most active in Wales. The son of King Selyf and St. Gwen (sister of St. Non), he was born around the year 483. Devout from his youth, he made a pilgrimage to Rome and Jerusalem while still young (probably in his early twenties), and on his way back to Cornwall was ordained a priest by the bishop of Poitiers.

On his return home, he learned that his father had died and he was now king. Not wanting to be tied to this world, he renounced his inheritance and traveled about Cornwall preaching, converting the pagans, and founding churches. But it seems that despite having abdicated the throne, he was pressured to reassume the crown, and so to avoid conflict he went to Wales accompanied by a small number of disciples.

When St. Cybi first arrived in Wales, King Edilig did not welcome him and tried to evict him and his party. But as Edilig approached him on horseback, his horse suddenly died and the king and all his men became blind. Edilig then prostrated himself before St. Cybi in sincere repentance, and immediately the sight of all was restored and the king's horse rose alive and well. Edilig then gave St. Cybi land on which to establish churches in Llangybi-ar-Wysg and Llanddyfrwyr-yn-Ediligion. Saint Cybi is patron saint of these two parishes today.

After he founded these churches, he resumed missionary activity in Ireland, spending four years in Aran. He later returned to Wales, this time settling on the Lleyn peninsula of Gwynedd, where he continued his efforts to spread the gospel of Christ. Impressed by his sanctity, Prince Maelgwn of Gwynydd gifted Cybi an abandoned Roman fort located on the island now called Ynys Gybi or Holy Island. In this former fort, St. Cybi established his most important monastery, called Caergybi, and became its abbot.

Saint Cybi developed a close friendship with St. Seiriol, a hermit who lived in a cell at Penmon on Anglesey. They would meet regularly at Llannerch-y-medd, roughly halfway between Penmon and Ynys Gybi. As he walked to their meeting place, St. Cybi faced the morning sun as he journeyed east and the afternoon sun as he returned west to Ynys Gybi. The result was that his face became quite tanned. Saint Seiriol, on the other hand, traveled for their meetings with the sun always at his back, so that the two were called Cybi Felyn and Seiriol Wyn (Cybi the Tanned and Seiriol the Fair). Meeting together near Llannerch-y-medd, they would drink from the Clorach well[55] and pray together. It was said that the prayers of Cybi and Seiriol protected the island.

Being renowned for his wisdom, St. Cybi was among those who attended the Synod at Llanddewi Brefi in 545[56] at which the Pelagian heresy was anathematized and St. David, according to his eleventh-century biographer Rhygyfarch, was proclaimed archbishop. Shortly afterward, the saint retired to Ynys Gybi, where he reposed peacefully on November 8, 555. He is commemorated on November 8.

There is a holy well not far from Llangybi church.[57] It is perhaps the most famous holy well in Lleyn. It is said that St. Cybi created the well by striking the ground with his staff. Many miracles have occurred through the waters of this well, and across the centuries it has been claimed to have aided in the healing of blindness, rheumatism, scrofula, and other maladies. The well is still visited today, and its waters are used often in baptisms.

Alternate spellings: Cuby, Kebi, Kebius

---

55   See https://wellhopper.wales/2016/10/15/clorach-wells/.
56   See also the chapters on St. David, St. Dyfrig, and St. Samson, who also were known to be present at this Synod.
57   See https://wellhopper.wales/2012/11/15/ffynnon-gybi-llangybi/.

St. David

The patron saint of Wales, St. David is without question the best known of all Welsh saints. Even so, many are confused by the fact that he is known by several different variations of his name, and the three most common are David, Dafydd, and Dewi. Certainly, the English version David is recognized universally, even among native Welsh speakers. The Welsh Dafydd is also quite popular in Wales itself. Yet often we see his name rendered Dewi, especially in churches that have been named after him. That is because Dewi is the form of David in southwestern Wales and is the name by which David is commonly known throughout the country. Rhygyfarch, the author of David's eleventh-century vita, wrote that he was baptized "Davidus" but that "the common people called him Dewi."[58]

Saint David was the son of St. Non, a virgin living in a monastic community at Ty Gwyn. (An account of his birth can be found in the life of St. Non on pages 66–68.) He was born around the year 500 in Pembrokeshire and was baptized at Porthclais by St. Ailbe, his first instructor in the Faith besides his mother.

As a small boy, David was sent to the monastery of Abbot Mawgan near Cardigan, where he was taught to read. He later became a monk at Ty Gwyn under St. Paul Aurelian while he was still quite young. David was ordained a priest, and he and St. Paul retired to a small island off the western coast of Wales in order to seek greater solitude. An angel soon thereafter appeared to St. Paul and instructed him to let David go into the world. Thus began David's missionary activity, a gift at which he excelled. Traveling throughout Wales, England, and Ireland, he founded a number of churches and monasteries. His zeal for the holy Faith was such that, in the words of Dmitry Lapa, he "filled the Welsh land with the spirit of holiness and asceticism,

---

58   Morgan, *In Pursuit of St. David*, 20.

providing the country with great spiritual potential and strength for many centuries."[59]

David's humility, devotion, and wisdom endeared him to all, and before long he was made abbot at Henllan, where he received an angelic vision that commanded him to go to a place called Glyn Rhosyn (now known as St. Davids/Ty Ddewi). There he founded his most famous monastery where many disciples gathered around him, including St. Padarn and St. Teilo. David and the monks practiced a very strict form of asceticism at Glyn Rhosyn. They did all the work themselves, not even using animals to plow the fields but relying entirely on their own labor. They worked together in total silence, had all possessions in common, practiced strict chastity, and ate nothing but vegetables and drank only water—hence David came to be called Dewi Ddyfrwr and Davidus Aquaticus ("David the Water-Drinker"). David's biographer Rhygyfarch described his monks as "living like the monks of Egypt."[60] David's monastic discipline was viewed as severe even by Celtic standards, and St. Gildas, writing a century later, himself recommended against such extremes, which he viewed as unduly harsh.

Nevertheless, a number of saints and saintly men came out of the monastery at Glyn Rhosyn and they preached Christ, converting countless pagans to Christianity throughout Wales, Cornwall, Devon, and Brittany. Numerous churches and villages can be found even today named after St. David, giving witness to the saint's effectiveness in spreading the gospel and validating his sobriquet as the "Apostle of Wales."[61]

One of the most famous miracles associated with St. David occurred when he spoke at the Council of Llanddewi Brefi.[62] Saint

---

59   Lapa, "Holy Hierarch David."
60   Gerald Morgan, 58.
61   Sterling, *St. David of Wales*, 10.
62   See also the chapters on St. Cybi, St. Dyfrig, and St. Samson, who also were present at this Synod.

Dyfrig had convened the council in 545 to condemn the heresy of Pelagianism, which was rampant in the Church in Britain at that time. Saint Dyfrig served as senior bishop, and during the conference he was asked to allow David to address the assembly, even though David was only a minor abbot. As David spoke, the ground rose up beneath him so that he could be seen and heard by everyone at the council. David's speech was so eloquent that St. Dyfrig decided to resign as senior bishop of the council in favor of David.

Saint David reposed peacefully in the Lord at Glyn Rhosyn sometime around 600. At the moment of his repose, the monastery was said to have been filled with angels. Some of his last words, recorded in his vita, were *"Gwnewch y pethau bychain mewn bywyd."* ("Do the little things in life," a maxim that is well known in Wales to this very day.) He was buried in the monastery church, but his relics later were translated to St. Davids Cathedral, where they share a casket with his confessor, Justinian.

Saint David is commemorated on March 1.

Alternate spellings: Dafydd, Davidus, Dewi

St. Derfel Gadarn

Saint Derfel Gadarn (Derfel the Valiant) was born around the year 466 and traditionally is believed to be a son of King Hywel of Brittany and brother of Ss. Tudwal and Arthfael. Legend has it that as a young man he was a soldier in King Arthur's army and was one of only seven to have survived the Battle of Camlann. If indeed he was a soldier during his early years, he later abandoned his soldierly ways and was drawn to a religious life. For a time he became a wandering hermit, but later he was a monk at Llanilltud Fawr on the coast of the Bristol Channel. At some point he established a church and monastic community at Llandderfel in Gwynedd.

Derfel's devotion became well known because he applied himself as assiduously to his religious duties in the Lord's army as he had as a warrior in his earlier life. He was chosen to be abbot of Ynys Enlli on Bardsey Island following the repose of his cousin St. Cadfan. He is believed to have reposed peacefully on April 5 or 6, 560, at a great old age.

A wooden statue of St. Derfel as a soldier on horseback (reminiscent of St. George fighting the dragon) was erected at Llandderfel and became a site of pilgrimage for many. It is said that the saint worked many miracles through this relic. Although the horse remains at Llandderfel to this day, the statue of St. Derfel came to a tragic end during Henry VIII's reign. In 1538 Thomas Cromwell had the image removed, despite protests, and brought to Smithfield, London, where it was dismantled and the wood used to burn to death a Roman Catholic priest named John Forest. This abominable act fulfilled an ancient prophecy that St. Derfel's image would someday burn down a forest.[63]

Saint Derfel Gadarn is commemorated on April 5.

Alternate spellings: Dervel, Dervell, Terbillius, Turville, Cadarn, Gdarn

St. Dyfrig (Dubricius)

Saint Dyfrig, who is referred to often by the Latinized name Dubricius, had God's special blessing from the moment he was born.

Dyfrig's grandfather was Peibo Clafrog, the king of Ergyng. After returning from a military campaign (circa 465), Peibo learned that his unwed daughter Erddyl was pregnant. Enraged by the news, he ordered that she be tied up in a bag and thrown into the River Wye, but instead of drowning, Erddyl was cast up onto the riverbank. This

---

63   Spencer, *Guide to the Saints of Wales,* 33.

process was repeated several times, but each time the river refused to accept her. Determined to get rid of the shame of an illegitimate birth, Peibo then ordered that Erddyl be burned alive. The following morning he sent a servant to the smoldering pyre to gather up her bones, but instead of finding bones the servant found Erddyl sitting quite unharmed and holding in her arms a newborn babe.

It became evident to Peibo that God's hand was at work in this affair, and thus he had Erddyl and the child brought to him. When he embraced them, the infant boy's hand touched Peibo's face and mouth, and immediately he was cured of a chronic frothing of the mouth from which he had long suffered. Peibo greatly rejoiced at this miraculous healing and his anger was turned into love for the boy, to the degree that he favored Dyfrig above his own sons and grandsons and declared him heir of the whole island of Ynys Erddyl (named after Dyfrig's mother).

When he was a young boy, Dyfrig was sent to an unnamed seminary, where he became known for his exceptional intellect. By the time he came of age he was recognized throughout Britain as an eminent scholar. He taught many great minds while he was at the seminary, and later he established a monastery and seminary in Henllan on the banks of the River Wye, into which his mother had been thrown years before. It is said that he had two thousand disciples at Henllan, among them Ss. Teilo, Cynfarch, and Samson.

After several years he returned to Ynys Erddyl along with his fellow monks to teach his native people. An angel appeared to him in a dream and instructed him to search about the island for a sow with piglets. At that place he was to build a monastery and seminary in the name of the Holy Trinity. The following day Dyfrig and his monks indeed found a place where a sow and her piglets lay, and there they laid the foundation of the monastery called Mochros (meaning "place of hogs"). From this place Dyfrig went about teaching the people, healing the sick, and establishing churches.

In 521 Dyfrig visited Llandaff Monastery, where he and St. Illtud consecrated Samson a deacon, priest, and bishop. Dyfrig and Illtud remained friends, and they, along with Ss. Samson and David, attended the Council of Llanddewi Brefi in 545.[64] At this council, Dyfrig served as senior bishop until he resigned in favor of St. David.

After leading his monastic flock for forty-three years, Dyfrig retired to Bardsey Island, where he became a hermit. He reposed peacefully in the Lord on Sunday, November 14, 612, and was buried on the island. In 1120 his relics were translated to Llandaff Cathedral, where there occurred during the procession a miracle of rain that ended a seven-week drought. In the course of preparing the saint's relics for reburial they were washed, and when Dyfrig's bones were placed in a basin the water began to boil and his arm bone moved on its own for an hour. The relics then were interred in a tomb before the altar of the Theotokos, where they remained until Henry VIII's Reformation.

Saint Dyfrig is commemorated on November 14.

Alternate spellings: Devereux, Dubric, Dubricius, Dubricus, Dyffrig

St. Gildas

Saint Gildas Badonicus[65] is believed to have been born around the year 494, but the place of his birth is unknown. Some think he was born in Scotland, others in northern England or Wales. What we do know is that as a young boy he was sent to Llanilltud Fawr to be educated by St. Illtud, where he became one of the saint's most beloved

---

64   See also the sections on St. Cybi, St. David, and St. Samson, who were also known to be present at this Synod.

65   The surname Badonicus was given because, as Gildas himself related, he was born at the time of the Battle of Badonicus when the Britons won a major victory over the Anglo-Saxons at Badon.

pupils. The author of the life of St. Paul Aurelian called Gildas "the brightest genius of the school of St. [Illtud],"[66] and he became known for his superb biblical knowledge. After completing his education at Llanilltud Fawr, Gildas went to Ireland, possibly accompanied by St. David, where he was ordained a priest. He became a highly effective teacher, converting many pagans and founding a number of churches throughout the land.

Gildas later returned to Wales, where he taught for a year at Llancarfan, the monastery that St. Cadoc founded. After that he made a pilgrimage to Rome, then came again to Wales in 537, settling on Ynys Echni (Flat Holm), a tiny island in the Bristol Channel. It was probably while staying here as a hermit that he wrote his most famous work, *De Excidio et Conquestu Britanniae* (*On the Ruin and Conquest of Britain*), a trilogy of homilies that gives a brief history of sub-Roman Britain and also a scathing denunciation of the country's leaders, both secular and religious, for their crimes and wantonness. In it he attributes the plundering of the country by the Picts and Scots, and later by the Saxons, as God's judgment upon the leaders' faithlessness. Although St. Gildas was renowned for his piety and compassion, he did not shrink from calling out those who would abuse their power, often by name, asking them to repent of their sins and embrace the Christian Faith.

Always one to value the benefits of solitude, in 544 St. Gildas went to Brittany and built a hermitage on the island of Houat in the Bay of Biscay near Vannes. Here he had hoped to spend his life in prayer and seclusion, but a group of fishermen discovered him. Impressed by the saint's sincere piety and holy conversation, they spread the news of his presence to the folk on the continent. Before long many people were venturing to Houat for instruction and advice from the holy one, and soon they compelled him to come to the continent and teach them

---

66   EWTN, "St. Gildas the Wise."

more formally. He finally agreed to this and moved to the mainland, establishing an oratory and monastery at Rhuys. After seeing to the monastery's establishment and writing a manual to help the abbots guide the brethren there, Gildas sought again a life of solitude and moved to a small cave on the bank of the river Blavet near Vannes.

Probably due to ill health, St. Gildas returned once more to Rhuys, where he reposed on January 29, 570. Rather than being buried, he had earlier requested that his body be placed in a boat and allowed to drift to where God would direct it. On May 11 of that year, the boat was found in a creek with the saint's body incorrupt. His body was taken to Rhuys and buried there, though it was moved to Berry in the tenth century. His relics were hidden in the cathedral at Vannes during the French Revolution, but they survived and have since been returned to Saint-Gildas-de-Rhuys, where they may be venerated today.

Saint Gildas is commemorated on January 29.

Alternate spellings: Gildas fab Caw, Gildas Sapiens (Gildas the Wise)

St. Non

The earliest life of St. Non that survives today was written about 500 years after her death by a Norman cleric named Rhygyfarch. It is principally from his *Life of St. David* that we know the most about Non and her honored son. Though as with most early Welsh saints accounts vary in details, it seems undeniable that Non was a saint chosen by God for marvelous things.

The daughter of Prince Cynyr Ceinfarfog, Non chose a religious life from youth and appears to have been a nun at Ty Gwyn where a monastic community existed. One day while on a pilgrimage, she was accosted by a local prince named Sant and was "unhappily seized and exposed to the sacrilegious violence" of being sexually assaulted.[67] The attack resulted in pregnancy.[68]

---

67 Stanton, *A Menology of England and Wales,* 99.
68 Some researchers believe the story of St. Non's ravishing by Sant is an invention of Rhygyfarch and that David was instead the legitimate son of

Non, who was celibate both before and after her attack, returned to her community where she likely endured much societal scorn since pregnancy outside of wedlock—for whatever cause—was viewed severely negatively at that time. She seems to have suffered her pregnancy and childbirth alone.

Once, as she was nearing time for the child to be born, she went to church to make an offering and to pray for a safe delivery.[69] A well-known and eloquent scholar[70] was preaching in the church that day, but when Non entered he suddenly stopped, unable to continue his homily. After a few minutes of embarrassing silence he explained to the congregants that he had not lost his voice but for some inexplicable reason was unable to continue to preach. He asked the people to go outside so he could see whether he would be able to preach when the building was empty. Everyone left except Non, who had secreted herself behind a pillar so that others would not see her shame of being pregnant and unmarried. Still the priest could not preach, so he cried out that someone must still be in the church and demanded they reveal themselves. Non then came out from behind the pillar, explaining that she hadn't wished to be seen by the others since she was unmarried but about to become a mother. The priest asked her to wait outside while the other people came back in. When she did so, the priest was able to complete his homily to the rest of the flock. When he finished he went outside and questioned Non. Learning her story, he then predicted that she would have a son who would be the most eloquent preacher in Britain and a great servant of God.

---

a chieftain in Ceredigion and related to the royal line of Gwynedd. The version of his conception and birth given here is nevertheless an account of long-standing tradition and has been generally accepted for generations as authentic.

69 This account also is given in the life of St. David (see pp. 57–60).

70 This possibly was St. Gildas.

When the time came for the child to be born, Non had to face the ordeal alone as no one was there to console her in her childbearing—very uncommon in that day not to have a midwife or other attendant present during childbirth. She went into labor at the place known today as Capel Non in Pembrokeshire. While she groaned in pain in an exceptionally difficult labor, it is said that a great storm thundered throughout the land except in the spot where she lay. There Non was bathed in light and utter calm. Nonetheless, the birth pangs were so severe that her fingers left marks on the rock where she grasped it, and at the moment of birth lightning struck the stone and split it in two in empathy with her.

Little is known of Non's later life, though it is clear that she brought up her son in the admonition of the Lord as he was to become one of the most revered and illustrious saints in the history of Wales—indeed, the patron saint of Wales. She went to Cornwall at some point, where she died sometime in the early sixth century. Her relics were venerated at Altarnum in Cornwall for several centuries but sadly were destroyed during the Reformation.

St. Non is commemorated on March 3.

Alternate spellings: Nemata, Nonna, Nonnet, Nonnita

St. Padarn

The exact date and place of Padarn's birth are not known. He is believed to have been born either in Wales or Brittany near the end of the fifth century. It is said that his father went to Ireland to pursue an ascetic life while Padarn was still quite young. When Padarn asked his mother whether his father was alive, she explained to him that he was indeed alive but that he had renounced the world and sought a life of prayer and meditation in Ireland. Inspired by his father's example, Padarn himself later traveled to Ireland as a young man to join his father in asceticism.

While he was in Ireland, Padarn joined his cousin St. Cadfan and a group of fellow monks on a journey to Wales. There Padarn became a student at St. Illtud's monastery at Llanilltud Fawr and later founded his own monastery at Llanbadarn Fawr near Aberystwyth. This became the seat of a new diocese, and Padarn was its first bishop.

At some point Padarn desired to visit his father again in Ireland and left the monastery in charge of others. When he arrived at his father's monastery, he found that two rival kings were at war with each other and were causing great devastation to the people of the area. As bishop, St. Padarn managed to get the two kings to negotiate a truce between them, and this accomplished a peace no one had previously believed possible.

When Padarn returned to Llanbadarn Fawr, he learned that King Maelgwn Gwynedd was attempting to cheat the monastery out of land that was properly theirs. The king sent two false witnesses, Graban and Terillan, to accuse St. Padarn of stealing royal treasure. They did this by filling large bags full of moss and gravel, which they then entrusted to Padarn's care until the king arrived, telling him that the bags were full of treasure. The saint faithfully watched after the hoard, never once touching it. When King Maelgwn arrived, his two henchmen came to collect the bounty from Padarn's cell and then opened the bags in front of the king. When only moss and gravel came out, they accused Padarn of having stolen the king's treasure and filling the bags with worthless dirt. By this means King Maelgwn intended to imprison Padarn and seize the monastery's lands in retribution for his theft.

At this time a peculiar method was in common practice, which alleged to reveal which of two parties was speaking the truth: Each would place a hand in boiling water, and the one whose hand was not burned would be revealed as the truth-teller. Saint Padarn requested that the king apply this method in his case, and when he placed his hand in the boiling water it remained unharmed and cold to the touch. When Graban and Terillan were compelled to place their hands likewise in the water, they both were severely scalded and shortly after fell dead. Theirs was not the only punishment God sent for the false accusations against the saint. King Maelgwn himself became blind and grew weak. Feeling himself about to die, he knelt before Padarn, confessed his treachery, and sought forgiveness. Padarn forgave him and prayed for the king's life to be spared and for his sight to be restored. This prayer was answered and the king, in gratitude and sincere penance, not only renounced any claim to the monastery's lands but instead gifted the monastery much more land.

Soon after these events, St. David received a heavenly vision in which an angel commanded him to make a pilgrimage to Jerusalem and to take with him Ss. Teilo and Padarn. While they were on this journey, God granted them the gift of tongues so that wherever they traveled the people of that region could understand their speech. Once in Jerusalem they were ordained bishops by the patriarch himself, thus overseeing the three episcopacies of Wales.

Accounts of St. Padarn's life diverge after this point. The twelfth-century vita tells of a trip to Brittany where he met with St. Samson and later died at Vannes. The vita also interweaves some Arthurian legends into the saint's life, which brings its credibility into question. It seems more likely that he remained at his bishopric in Llanbadarn Fawr until retiring to Bardsey Island, where he reposed and was buried around the year 550.

Saint Padarn is commemorated on April 15.

Alternate spellings: Padarnus, Padern, Patern, Paternus,

St. Paul Aurelian

As there have been many saints who have borne the name St. Paul throughout history—many living concurrently with one another—St. Paul Aurelian is sometimes confused with other saints of the same name. Our St. Paul is frequently referred to as St. Paulinus of Whitby, St. Pawlhen, or other variations (see below). While no vita of the saint survives, we know a fair amount about his life from accounts of other saints—particularly St. David and St. Teilo—as he was deeply instrumental in their education and spiritual development. He had a profound influence on the lives of many saints and other faithful people of his era.

Saint Paul Aurelian was the son of a British chieftain and was born in the late fifth century near Llandovery. Deeply devoted to spiritual pursuits from his youth, he became a monk and later a student of St. Illtud. Rhygyfarch's *Life of St. David* also describes him as a disciple of St. Garmon (Germanus).

Paul Aurelian demonstrated prodigious advancement in knowledge and wisdom under St. Illtud and went on to found a monastery at Whitland, where he served as abbot. He guided the monks there by encouraging much prayer, study, and devotion. Several of these young monks went on to become saints themselves, among them St. Teilo of Llandaff and St. David of Wales. Paul Aurelian was highly sought after for instruction in the monastic life, and he was equally dedicated to spreading the gospel of Christ among the people of Wales. He is thought to have established a number of churches in and around Llandovery.

In his old age, St. Paul Aurelian began losing his sight so that he found ordinary activities increasingly difficult to perform, especially reading and teaching. His condition progressed so that one day he awoke unable to see at all. His beloved student, the young St. David, came to him and touched his eyelids, praying that God would restore his sight. When St. Paul opened his eyes, he found that his sight indeed had been restored. It was this event that likely revealed to him how important this young student was to the future of the Church in Wales. And it was St. Paul Aurelian who convinced St. David to address the council at Llanddewi Brefi a little later.

Saint Paul Aurelian died at a very advanced age around the year 575, but his influence on the spiritual development of the Church in Wales transcends time. A sixth-century stone from Cynwyl Gaeo parish, which can be found now in the Carmarthen Museum, is inscribed with these words in the saint's honor: "Preserver of the faith, constant lover of his country, champion of righteousness."[71]

Saint Paul Aurelian is commemorated on November 23.

Alternate spellings: Paul Hen, Paulinus, Pawlhen, Peulin, Pewlin, Polin

---

71   Catholic.net, "St. Paul Aurelian."

St. Petroc

Saint Petroc was born around 468, the third child of King Glywys of Glywysing. Devoted to the religious life from childhood, he went with a small number of companions to Ireland when he came of age, and there he lived for about twenty years, studying at various monasteries. Having embraced ascetic discipline in Ireland, the group later decided to return to their homeland. When they went to the shore to embark on their journey back to Wales, they found the same ship they had used to travel to Ireland more than two decades earlier. Miraculously, the ship was in the same condition it had been in on their initial voyage, and they took this as an indication of God's approval of their decision to return.

Sailing eastward, the group came to Trebetherick in Cornwall, where they sensed God had led them. Once Petroc and his disciples disembarked, they met some peasants reaping in a nearby field. Greeting them courteously and asking how they were, they answered Petroc rather rudely because they were suspicious of these oddly clad monastics. The reapers mocked Petroc, and in reply to his inquiry they said only that they were very thirsty and would be happy to see a spring of water gush forth from a rock there in the field. Petroc then prayed and struck the rock with his staff, and just as had happened with Moses in the wilderness water sprang out from the rock. At such a miracle, the peasants were immediately convinced that these indeed were God-fearing men, and they gave praise to the Lord. Petroc asked whether there were other religious men in the area, and they told him about St. Samson, a hermit who was then staying in a nearby cell devoting himself to much prayer and fasting.

Petroc hastened to St. Samson's cell where Samson told Petroc of another Christian hermit in the area named Wethnoc. When Wethnoc observed Petroc's exceptional piety, he offered his own cell to him, asking that Petroc establish a monastery at that place and name it Llanwethinoc (now known as Padstow). Petroc honored this request and founded a church and monastery there. Wethnoc then moved on from there, giving thanks to God for having been allowed to prepare a place for Petroc and his disciples. Petroc took up habitation in Wethnoc's former cell and lived there while serving as abbot of Llanwethinoc for thirty years.

At length, Petroc decided to go on a pilgrimage to Rome along with several fellow monks. On their return they encountered a fierce storm as they traveled along the roads in north Devon. Petroc's companions began to grumble and complain about the conditions, but he assured them to take heart, as the storm would soon abate and they would have fair weather the next day. When morning dawned, however, the storm was as fierce as ever, and from this Petroc realized he had been guilty of prelest,[72] having spoken as though his words were from God when in fact he was merely stating his own will. In humble repentance for this presumption, Petroc turned again to make another pilgrimage to Rome, this time in penance for being a false prophet. Only after his second trip to Rome did Petroc return again to Cornwall.

Following this long double journey, Petroc began to feel the infirmities of age and the need for a rest from the duties of an abbot. He therefore secretly went to Little Petherick, along with two brothers from the monastery, in order to recover his strength. After spending fifteen days there, he grew concerned about the brothers at the monastery who had been left wondering what had happened to their abbot, and so he went again to Llanwethinoc to let the disciples there know where he had gone and to tell them it was time for him to hand over the oversight of the monastery to others.

After he ordained his successor, Petroc withdrew again to Little Petherick, along with twelve brothers who elected to remain under

---

72 Spiritual delusion or pride.

his spiritual guidance. The brothers there lived in separate cells but would gather together for meals and prayer. The place had one deficiency, and that was a lack of water. As this caused the brothers to suffer unduly, Petroc prayed to God and then thrust his staff into the ground outside his cell. Immediately a spring of water gushed from the ground. The water was so abundant that in addition to a chapel the brothers built a mill at Little Petherick.

After a time Petroc desired even greater solitude and withdrew to Bodmin, where he became a hermit, taking up residence in a cell St. Guron had recently vacated when he relocated to Gorran Haven. At Bodmin, Petroc continued in fasting and prayer but, like most hermits of his day, he also traveled regularly, preaching Christ, converting the pagans, and strengthening the brethren.

As Petroc was nearing the end of his life, he desired to visit his disciples at Llanwethinoc one last time. As he was journeying there, he stayed one night in the farmhouse of a family named Rovel. Already suffering from old age and disease, he grew weaker during the night and asked to receive the Eucharist from his companions. Afterward, on the night of June 4, 564, he reposed quietly. He was buried at Bodmin.

Saint Petroc is commemorated on June 4.

Alternate spellings: Perreux, Petrocus, Petrog, Petrox

St. Samson

Although known as St. Samson of Dol (Brittany), Samson was born and educated in Wales. We are blessed to know a great deal about his life because—unlike most Welsh saints of the early centuries—his *Vita Sancti Samsonis*, written not long after his death, still survives.

Samson's parents were wealthy nobles, Amon of Dyfed and Anna of Gwent. Like Joachim and Anna, Zacharias and Elizabeth, and Abraham and Sarah, Amon and Anna were childless for many years. When at last Anna discovered she was pregnant with Samson, she and Amon saw it as a sign from God. Therefore, when Samson was only five years old (around the year 491, thus having been born around 486) he was sent to Llanilltud Fawr to be nurtured in the Faith by the great St. Illtud. It is said that even at so young an age, he himself greatly desired to live at this monastery and learn the ways of holy living.

As a student, young Samson excelled in all his studies. After being taught the alphabet, he was able, by the grace of God, to read after a mere seven days. He quickly mastered all the psalms, outshining all his fellow students in knowledge and understanding of the Holy Scriptures. He grew equally strong in the spirit of monasticism. By age fifteen he was known for his frequent fasts and lengthy vigils in which he exercised himself to the point that his master admonished him to relax some of his self-imposed disciplines so that he did not bring harm to his physical body.

One summer morning a group of the brethren went into the fields to pull weeds out of the crops when one of the brothers was bitten by a viper. He fell to the ground, severely affected by the poison so that the other brothers feared for his life. They sent word to the abbot, St. Illtud, who at the time was instructing the young Samson in his lessons. When Samson heard what had happened, he wept for the brother and begged his master to allow him to go to the suffering monk. Permitted to go, Samson found the brother near death. Samson made the sign of the cross over the wound and prayed earnestly for the brother's healing, and within three hours the brother recovered completely.

All the brethren greatly regarded and loved Samson, but to guard himself against falling into pride he increased his ascetic labors. When he reached manhood, he was ordained a deacon and shortly thereafter a priest, while at Llanilltud Fawr. During his ordination a white dove perched on a beam above him and remained unflinching throughout the ordination. When St. Dyfrig raised his hand over Samson to confirm him as a deacon, the dove came and landed on Samson's shoulder and would not fly away until the entire ceremony had been completed.

Although Samson's exemplary life of asceticism won him the love and affection of his monastic companions, Satan entered the hearts of two of the brothers who became increasingly envious of him. They became so overcome with jealousy that they conspired to poison Samson. To ensure that the poison was indeed effective, they placed some of it in a bowl of milk and gave it to the monastery cat. On drinking it, the cat leapt forward in pain and immediately fell dead. But when they gave a poisoned cup to Samson he received it gladly, made the sign of the cross over it, and drank it dry without suffering any harmful consequences. Instead, he complimented the brother for serving him such a refreshing drink that brought "sweetness to [his] throat" and "strength to [his] heart."[73]

Since God had certainly preserved the life of Samson (as Christ had said of His faithful, "If they drink anything deadly, it will by no means hurt them" [Mark 16:18]), one of the cunning brothers was stricken in his heart and reproved his accomplice who had lured him into the deed in the first place. The evil brother, however, did not deplore his sin but allowed the worm of resentment to grow inside him. The following Sunday when he received the Holy Eucharist from the hand of the man he hated, suddenly he turned pale, began belching and trembling, and thrashed about as one mad. When the repentant brother witnessed this, he openly confessed their sin to all and pledged henceforth to serve God and Samson faithfully.

After a time Samson decided to seek even greater ascetic austerity and went to the island monastery of Caldey off the coast of Dyfed.

---

73   Taylor, *Life of St. Samson*, 24.

Here he humbled himself to be the cellarer.[74] One day Pyro, the abbot of the monastery, consumed too much wine and fell into a well and drowned. After this Samson, who abstained entirely from alcohol, was elected abbot. He served as abbot faithfully for three years, then on learning that his father had become gravely ill, Samson took leave of the monastery and went to his father's side.

Finding Amon on his deathbed, Samson persuaded his father to become a monk before he died. Amon accepted the monastic tonsure and was immediately healed of his illness. Witnessing this, many of their relatives promptly followed Amon's example and accepted the monastic life themselves.

After Samson returned to Caldey as abbot, word of his sanctity and devotion grew. One day a group of Irish pilgrims passed through Caldey on their way back from Rome. Having learned that the pilgrims were monks and scholars, Samson chose to travel with them to Ireland, where he stayed a short while. According to his vita, he performed many miracles while in Ireland including curing lepers, restoring sight to the blind, and casting out demons. Through his preaching he converted many pagans to Christ.

When he returned to Wales, the brothers begged him to resume serving as their abbot, but instead he chose to retire from oversight of the monastery and, with his father and a small number of other brothers, became a hermit on the banks of the River Severn. Here, after making sure his companions had appropriate dwellings, he then sought yet deeper isolation for himself and left to take up residence in a small cave that faced the east and had a spring beside it.

Around the year 521, Samson had a vision of himself serving at the altar with Ss. Peter, James, and John. They informed Samson that they had been sent to confirm that he was soon to become a bishop.

---

74   The person in charge of maintaining the necessary supply of food and drink in a monastery.

The following night St. Dyfrig also received a vision of an angel, who instructed him to make Samson a bishop, as it was pleasing to God. When Dyfrig consecrated Samson as bishop, he and others serving the Liturgy witnessed the appearance of a dove, just as one had come when he was ordained a deacon.

One year as he was preparing to serve the Paschal Liturgy, Samson readied himself by keeping an all-night vigil standing alone at the altar, as was his custom. During that night a mighty angel appeared to him and, after bidding him to be of good cheer and not to be afraid, instructed him that he should not tarry further in Wales but that God had ordained that he become a pilgrim beyond the sea in Brittany. So after completing the Paschal Liturgy, the next day Samson began making his way toward his new calling. As he passed through Cornwall with several companions, Samson performed more miracles, converted many pagans, and met St. Petroc. Even after he began sailing across the Channel, Samson's missionary fire could not be quenched, and he stopped for a time on the island of Guernsey and converted the entire island to Christ.

When he finally arrived in Brittany, he established his most famous monastery at Dol, which he made his center of activity. He arrived at a time when the region was experiencing a great deal of political unrest. It seems that the legitimate king had been assassinated by the usurper Conomor, and another adversary (King Childebert I of the Franks) had taken the rightful Briton heir, Judual, captive. Samson went to King Childebert to appeal to him to release Judual. When Samson healed a demon-possessed member of Childebert's court, the king not only freed Judual but awarded Samson with land for his monastery and nominated him to be ordained bishop of Dol. Once Judual had been released from captivity, Samson excommunicated the evil King Conomor. This allowed Judual to assume his rightful place on the throne. Later, when Samson attended the Third Church Council in Paris in 557 (where he signed a document with his own hand, signing it "Samson, a sinner"[75]), he was conse-crated bishop of Dol.

Saint Samson performed many more miracles during his time in Brittany. He is said to have reposed peacefully in the Lord in 565, the brothers surrounding his bed hearing choirs of angels singing as his soul departed. He was buried in the cathedral in Dol, and in the tenth century King Æthelstan of England obtained his arm and a cro-zier, and they were placed in the Milton Abbas Monastery in Dorset. Some of his relics are still preserved at Dol and also in Caldey Abbey in Wales.

Saint Samson is commemorated on July 28.

Alternate spellings: Sampson, Samsun

St. Seiriol

It is not known when St. Seiriol was born or died, but he was a con-temporary of St. Cybi (circa 483–555), as the two were very close friends. The youngest son of King Owain Danwyn of Rhos, Seiriol became a hermit at Penmon on Anglesey, where he created a small "beehive" cell. Near the cell was a holy well from which he and his monks would drink and perform baptisms, and the well still exists today.[76]

It is very likely, though not known for certain, that like many other Welsh saints of the sixth century St. Seiriol left his cell on occasion to travel on missionary journeys throughout the region, using his humble cell as a home base. A monastic community gathered around him, and it is said that his brothers rebuilt his cell because they felt it was so meager that it was inadequate for habitation. The monks

---

75   Lapa, "Saint Samson of Dol."
76   Davis, *Sacred Springs*, 105–107.

SANT
SEIRIOL WYN

SANT
CYBI FELYN

eventually built a monastery that became one of the principal monasteries in Wales (it was sacked by Vikings in 971).

In his old age St. Seiriol retired to a hermitage on Ynys Seiriol (known today as Puffin Island), which was even more remote than Penmon, where a small monastery was established. This is probably where the saint reposed, though the exact place and date of his death are unknown.

Saint Seiriol is commemorated on February 1.

St. Teilo

Although Teilo was a close friend (perhaps even a cousin) and disciple of St. David, we know far less about him than about David. Born around the year 500 in Penally, Dyfed, Teilo is believed to have been a son of Ensich ap Hydwn, a relative of Ss. Isfael and Euddogwy. Moved by intense devotion to the Holy Church, he reportedly gave away all his possessions and sought a monastic life during his youth. He was educated by St. Paul Aurelian at Whitland and by St. Dyfrig at Henllan. While he was a student at Whitland, Teilo met St. David and the two became close friends.

Once he had acquired the discipline of monasticism, Teilo founded the monastery of Llandeilo Fawr in Dyfed, which became the principal center of Welsh monasticism and remained so for centuries. At some point he was ordained bishop of Llandaff, where he continued to instruct the people, and it is said that at its peak there were a thousand monks studying under Teilo at Llandaff.

When the Plague of Justinian[77] came to Wales in the 540s, St. Teilo and a small group of monks went to Dol in Brittany for about seven years. While they were there, Teilo met St. Samson and the two

---

77 The Plague of Justinian (541–549) was a pandemic that killed an estimated 15 to 100 million people as it spread from the Mediterranean Basin to Western Europe.

helped plant large fruit groves in the area, some of which remain to this day and are known even now as the groves of Teilo and Samson.

Several miracles are attributed to St. Teilo while he was in Brittany. At the behest of King Budic II, the saint subdued a winged dragon (likely a demon) that had been tormenting the local populace. Teilo tamed it and tied it to a rock in the sea. On another occasion he cast out a demon from a nobleman's castle. And when he was subsequently offered as much land as he could traverse between sunrise and sunset, he miraculously tamed a wild stag and rode on it in order to cover a much larger area than he could have done on foot.

Saint Teilo returned to Wales around 554 along with St. Euddogwy and other disciples, taking up residence once again at Llandeilo Fawr. He reposed peacefully at the monastery on February 9 around the year 560.

One of the most famous miracles surrounding St. Teilo occurred after his death. A dispute arose between the churches at Penally, Llandeilo Fawr, and Llandaff over where the saint's relics should be preserved. All three desired the honor. Penally claimed him because it was the place of his birth; Llandeilo Fawr because it was the monastery he had founded and where he died; and Llandaff because he had served as their bishop. Rather than allowing the dispute to cause friction between them, the monks all prayed fervently that God's will would be done. During the night the saint's body miraculously multiplied itself so that all three claimants could enshrine his remains.

Saint Teilo is the patron saint of the Welsh capitol city of Cardiff, and still today there is a holy well dedicated to him in Llandaff.[78] He is commemorated on February 9.

Alternate spellings: Eilliau, Eliau, Elios, Teleau, Teliarus, Teliau, Telo

---

[78] See https://britishlistedbuildings.co.uk/300013717-st-teilos-well-llandaff.

SEVENTH CENTURY

St. Beuno

Saint Beuno is believed to have been born at Berriew in Powys sometime in the latter half of the sixth century. Like many early Welsh saints he is said to have been of royal descent, the brother of Gwenlo, wife of Tyfid ap Eiludd, and therefore uncle to St. Gwenfrewy. Beuno was educated in the monastery at Bangor (though some sources say he was a colleague of Cadog at Caerwent), and after being ordained priest he founded a monastery at Llanfeuno in Ewyas (now Monmouthshire).

When he learned that his father was deathly ill, Beuno returned to Powys and established a small monastic community in Berriew. One day when he was walking along the River Severn he heard a man calling his dogs in the Saxon language. Alarmed by this, Beuno gathered his disciples and told them that they must leave this place, "for the nation of the man with an alien tongue will invade it."[79]

Moving westward, Beuno settled on the banks of the River Dee in ancient Gwynedd, where King Cadwallon granted him land. Trouble developed between Beuno and Cadwallon, however, and in order to avoid political intrigue and injustice Beuno went to Clynnog Fawr, where his brother-in-law, Tyfid ap Eiludd, gave him land on which to

---

79   J. B. Davies, *Saints of Wales,* 25.

establish his most renowned monastery. In gratitude for this gift of land, Beuno offered to become the spiritual father to Tyfid's daughter, St. Gwenfrewy, and educated her in the Faith. It is his intervention in restoring Gwenfrewy back to life that is perhaps the best remembered incident of Beuno's life (see pages 89–92).

Saint Beuno was abbot of the monastery at Clynnog Fawr and was also St. Gwenfrewy's spiritual father. He performed a number of miracles of healing and became quite well known for his knowledge of the Holy Scriptures. After he left Clynnog Fawr, he traveled as a missionary throughout Wales, southwest England, and possibly also Ireland. He founded at least nine monasteries during his lifetime, all of which became acclaimed centers of learning and devotion. In his later years he returned to Clynnog Fawr, where he reposed peacefully a few days after Pascha in 640 or 645 and was buried. A number of miracles was reported to have occurred at his grave, and after his body was translated to Eglwys y Bedd in Holywell many other miracles continued to occur. Saint Beuno is the patron saint of sick children and sick cattle to this day.

Saint Beuno is commemorated on April 21.

Alternate spellings: Bono, Bonus

St. Euddogwy (Oudoceus)

Often referred to as St. Oudoceus, most of what we know of the life of this saint appears in the twelfth-century *Book of Llandaff* and in *The Life of St. Oudoceus.*

His story begins with his father, Budic the son of Cybydan of Cornouaille in Brittany. As a young nobleman, Budic was expelled from his native country and went into exile in Wales. There he married Anawfedd, a daughter of Ensic and relative of St. Teilo. While in exile they had two sons, and Anawfedd was pregnant with her third child when Budic was called back to Brittany to assume the throne of Amorica, left vacant by the death of their king. Euddogwy was born shortly after their return to Brittany (around the year 540), and in gratitude for his family's restoration to his homeland Budic commended his son to God.

The young Euddogwy was sent to be educated at Llanilltud Fawr, where he excelled in his studies as well as in humility and sanctity. His knowledge and virtue became so well known that he was elected bishop of Llandaff, a position he held in great honor for many years. At one point he went on a pilgrimage to St. Davids, carrying with him a chest containing the relics of some of St. Teilo's late disciples. While they were traveling through the country, some bandits who assumed the chest they carried was full of treasure set upon him and his brothers. But before they could reach out and take the chest or raise their lances against the saint, they were struck blind and their arms became stiff so that they could not move.

Seeing this miracle, St. Euddogwy fell to his knees to petition God on the robbers' behalf, remembering what the Lord had spoken through the Prophet Ezekiel: "I have no pleasure in the death of the wicked, but that the wicked turn from his way and live" (Ezek. 33:11). God heard the saint's prayer and restored sight and movement to the bandits, who in turn repented before Euddogwy, vowing to devote their lives henceforth to fasting, prayer, and obedience to the Holy Church.

On another occasion St. Euddogwy was in devotion near the River Wye. Becoming warm, he removed his outer cloak and laid it on the ground. Not far away, King Einion and a group of companions were hunting stag in the forest. They and their dogs swiftly pursued a large stag that ran to the place where the saint was. Out of breath, the stag lay on the saint's cloak, and having done so the dogs chasing him suddenly became mute and refused to go any closer. King Einion and his fellow hunters were so astonished by this occurrence that they came to St. Euddogwy and on their knees begged forgiveness as though they had committed a terrible crime. The king then gave St. Eud-dogwy possession of the stag, now tame, and also gave to him and his brothers all the territory through which he and his men had pursued the beast.

Saint Euddogwy later retired to this land, being full of years, and built a residency and oratory for himself and his disciples. In his remaining years he lived in quiet devotion with his brethren, giving aid to any who came to him for paternal counsel or any other need. He gave special attention to the needs of widows and orphans who ventured his way. It is said that many other miracles were performed through this righteous saint but that only a few were written down.

Saint Euddogwy reposed peacefully in the Lord on July 2, some-time around the year 615. He is commemorated on July 2.

Alternate spellings: Oudoceus, Ouduck

St. Gwenfrewy (Winefride/Winifred)

Saint Gwenfrewy (more commonly known in English as St. Winifred) was born around the year 600 in Tegeingl (modern-day Flintshire). She was the daughter of Tyfid ap Eiludd, a Welsh noble, and Gwenlo, a sister of St. Beuno.

Her story actually begins with her uncle. When St. Beuno was first abbot of the monastery in Clynnog, he was troubled by local princes. To escape their political meddling, he sought refuge with his sister's husband, Tyfid, who granted him land near their estate.[80] Here St. Beuno built a church and agreed to be Gwenfrewy's teacher. Saint Beuno had a profound effect on Gwenfrewy, and even as a small child she greatly admired him, especially his deep devotion to the Lord. She herself decided at a young age that she wished to dedicate herself to God and become a nun.

---

80   See the section on St. Beuno, pp. 85–86.

One Sunday as St. Beuno served the Liturgy while the rest of the family was in attendance, Gwenfrewy was at home by herself.[81] As it happened, a Prince Caradoc was traveling through the area and stopped at Tyfid's house to ask for a drink of water. When Gwenfrewy obliged, Caradoc was smitten by her physical beauty and proposed that she become his wife. Desiring to preserve her virginity for Christ, she declined his proposal. Not one to accept rejection, Caradoc became indignant and attempted to take Gwenfrewy by force. She escaped his clutches and ran toward the church for asylum, but Caradoc on horseback quickly overcame her as she approached the church steps. He again tried to force himself on her, but when she continued to resist he angrily drew his sword and in his fury beheaded her.

By this time the people in the church had heard the commotion and came outside to see what was the matter. Seeing Gwenfrewy's lifeless body and Caradoc haughtily wiping her blood from his sword, St. Beuno sternly rebuked Caradoc for his unholy deed. At that Caradoc fell dead on the spot—some accounts say that the ground opened and swallowed him whole, others that demons came and snatched away his body. Saint Beuno then picked up Gwenfrewy's head and placed it back on her body. Then he and the whole church prayed that God would restore the innocent young maiden to life. When they all rose from their prayer, St. Gwenfrewy rose with them, her head and life restored, but retaining a red mark around her neck. This mark stayed with her the rest of her life as a remembrance of her miraculous revival.

After being given back her life, Gwenfrewy sat with Beuno on a rock (known today as St. Beuno's Rock), and Beuno said that anyone seeking help through Gwenfrewy's prayers "would obtain the

---

81   This account is also found in the section on St. Beuno.

grace he asked if it was for the good of his soul."[82] At the place where Gwenfrewy's head had fallen, a well of healing water sprang forth. It is known today as St. Winifred's Well at Holywell and remains one of the most sacred sites in all of Wales.[83]

For the next eight years, St. Gwenfrewy remained at Holywell, Flintshire, receiving instruction from St. Beuno and gathering around her eleven other virgins who, like herself, chose to dedicate their lives to God in celibacy. When St. Beuno eventually left Holywell to help evangelize other parts of Wales, St. Gwenfrewy made a pilgrimage to Rome, where she learned about monastic life. She found it to be somewhat different from traditional monastic life in Wales, where monastic communities tended to be more eremitic in structure, following the example of the Desert Fathers of Egypt. In Rome she observed a more cenobitic monasticism and saw a number of benefits from such an arrangement. When she returned to Wales, she called together a synod (known as the "Synod of Winifred") to discuss changing monastic life in Wales to the cenobitic style, as it would be much safer, especially for women, than living in solitary fashion as had been the custom.

Saint Gwenfrewy went to Gwytherin, where her cousin St. Eleri lived, and together with Eleri's mother, St. Tenoi, the three established a double monastery in cenobitic style, St. Eleri overseeing the men and St. Tenoi the women. When Tenoi reposed, St. Gwenfrewy became abbess of the women's monastery there.

After devoting the whole of her life (or "both lives," as it were) to the service of Christ and His Church, Gwenfrewy reposed peacefully in the Lord at Gwytherin on November 3, 660. She is thus commemorated on November 3.

---

82   New Advent, "St. Winefride."

83   Davis, 76–80.

In addition to the famous holy well at Holywell, there is also a Winifred's Well in Shropshire. It is said that as her body was being translated from Gwytherin to Shrewsbury Abbey, the attendants stopped to rest for the night at a spot near Woolston in Shropshire. When they lifted her body to continue the journey the next morning, another holy well sprang up out of the ground at the place where she had lain. Both holy wells are still extant near Woolston.

Alternate spellings: Gwenffrewi, Wenefreda, Winefride, Winifred, Winnefride

St. Melangell

Saint Melangell is among the few early Welsh saints whose memory has been commemorated consistently throughout the centuries. Even during the days of Henry VIII's Reformation, when so much destruction of religious objects connected with the saints took place, the locals hid the shrine and reliquary of St. Melangell so that they survived. The influence of her life is felt to this day in the area of Cwm Pennant.

Although the earliest surviving written accounts of St. Melangell's life were written about nine hundred years after her death, the degree to which she has been venerated throughout the centuries lends credence to the likelihood of their authenticity. According to most accounts, Melangell was a seventh-century princess in Ireland and worshipper of the Lord Christ. Betrothed through an arranged marriage, she wanted instead to preserve her virginity in a life of asceticism. She therefore fled from her home in Ireland to a remote spot in Wales known today as Pennant Melangell. Here she found a small cave that became her cell, where she lived in much the same way as the Desert Fathers. She lived in solitude in this place for fifteen years, devoting herself to prayer and ascetic struggles.

Y SANTES MELANGELL

One day Prince Brochwel Ysgithrog of Powys was hunting in the forest near Pennant. He and his dogs were pursuing a hare when his dogs suddenly stopped giving chase. The hare had sought refuge beneath the hem of a young virgin praying in a clearing. Astonished by the sight and smitten by the woman's beauty, Brochwel approached Melangell to learn more about her. After hearing her history and how she had lived there alone for the last fifteen years, Brochwel was deeply moved by her sincere devotion. Seeing her as a true servant of God, he gave her the surrounding lands to be a refuge in perpetuity. Brochwel stated that "if any men or women flee hither to seek thy protection . . . let no prince or chieftain be so rash towards God as to attempt to drag them forth."[84]

News of the holy Melangell spread, and before long a number of other chaste women came to Pennant, where a small religious community was established with Melangell as abbess. These women lived in quiet piety for thirty-seven years under the guidance of Melangell, who reposed around the year 670.

The sanctity of the area remained long after St. Melangell's presence there, and the prince's admonition that no one should disturb those who dwelt there stayed in effect. It is said that after Melangell died, a wicked man named Elise came to Pennant with the intention of defiling the virgins living there. His plans, however, were divinely foiled and he died a most horrible death.

To this very day, the locals dare not kill a hare, in reverence to how St. Melangell cared for creatures of its kind. It has long been customary that when local residents see a hare being pursued by dogs they cry out, *"Duw a Melangell a'th gadwo!"* ("God and Melangell preserve thee!")[85]

Saint Melangell is commemorated on May 27.

---

84   McLees, "Melangell with a Thousand Angels."
85   McLees.

St. Tysilio

Saint Tysilio was born sometime before 560, the youngest son of Brochwel Ysgithrog[86] and Arddyn Benasgel, king and queen of Powys. His father appears to have died when Tysilio was very young, and from a young age the boy exhibited a deep devotion to God and to the Holy Church. While likely still in his teens, Tysilio entered the monastery at Meifod and became a monk under the spiritual direction of Gwyddfarch, the founder and abbot of the monastery. While living at this monastery, Tysilio became friends with the young St. Beuno.

In time he received the blessing of Gwyddfarch to lead a more solitary life in prayer, and he went to a small island (now known as Ynys Dysilio) near Anglesey, where he lived as an anchorite for seven years. Like many other monastics of that period in Wales, Tysilio did not separate himself entirely from society but went about preaching the gospel, aiding the poor, and establishing churches. He ventured mostly around the area of Anglesey, but he also traveled well beyond the area and founded churches throughout Wales. The village of Llandysilio even today is named in his honor. He came to be widely respected as both a scholar and pious teacher whose life emulated Christ in every way. (As a point of interest, the village in Wales famous for having the longest name, Llanfairpwll-gwyngyllgogerychwyrndrobwllllantysiliogogogoch, is where one of St. Tysilio's churches still stands, its name incorporated into the place name itself.)

Saint Tysilio returned to Meifod after his time in Ynys Dysilio, and when Gwyddfarch died Tysilio was elected abbot in his place. In addition to administering the monastery, Tysilio continued his missionary activity as well, instructing the people and founding churches.

---

86   The same prince who discovered St. Melangell (see p. 92).

At some point after becoming abbot of Meifod, Tysilio's elder brother died, and his widow wanted Tysilio to abandon his vow of celibacy and marry her so that he might become the king of Powys. Evidently, she was quite persistent in this and caused the saint much annoyance, but he refused to abdicate his higher calling.

Some accounts say that St. Tysilio went to Brittany late in life—perhaps to escape the unrelenting attentions of his widowed sister-in-law—though whether he did so is unclear. He is believed to have reposed around the year 640, either in Brittany or in Meifod. No shrine is known to have contained his relics, but a holy well was dedicated to him in Guilsfield, Powys.

Saint Tysilio is commemorated on November 8.

Alternate spellings: Suliac, Sulian, Suliau, Tyssilo, Tysilius, Tyssel

APPENDIX 1

Welsh Saints by Century

First Century
St. Cyllin
St. Eigen
St. Ilid

Second Century
St. Deruvian
St. Ffagan
St. Tyfanog

Third Century
St. Amphibalus
St. Caron

Fourth Century
St. Elen
St. Elledeyrn
St. Germanus (Garmon)
St. Mellon

Fifth Century
St. Adwen ferch Brychan

St. Brioc
St. Brychan
St. Cadoc
St. Callwen ferch Brychan
St. Clydwyn ap Brychan
St. Cynheiddon (Endelienta)
    ferch Brychan
St. Cynog ap Brychan
St. Cystennin
St. Digain
St. Dilic ferch Brychan
St. Dingad ap Brychan
St. Dochau
St. Dochelin
St. Dogfan ap Brychan
St. Dogmael
St. Drichan
St. Dwynwen ferch Brychan
St. Dyfnan ap Brychan
St. Eigron
St. Eiliwedd ferch Brychan
St. Elian

St. Erbin

St. Ffinian

St. Garmon (Garmanus)

St. Gwen ferch Brychan

St. Gwen ferch Cynyr

St. Gwenfyl ferch Brychan

St. Gwladys ferch Brychan

St. Gwrhai

St. Gwynllyw

St. Henwg

St. Illtud

St. Illudiana

St. Ina

St. Keyne ferch Brychan

St. Kywere

St. Llawddog

St. Llionio

St. Mabyn ferch Brychan

St. Madrun (Materiana)

St. Maël

St. Mawgan

St. Menefrida ferch Brychan

St. Morwenna ferch Brychan

St. Nectan ap Brychan

St. Peblig

St. Tathyw

St. Tedda

St. Tybie

St. Tydfil ferch Brychan

St. Umbrafel

St. Veep

Sixth Century

St. Afan

St. Almadha

St. Aneurin

St. Armael (Arthfael)

St. Asaph

St. Athan

St. Austell

St. Baglan

St. Barrwg (Barry)

St. Bidofydd

St. Briavel

St. Brynach

St. Budoc

St. Cadfan

St. Cadfarch

St. Caffo

St. Canna

St. Carannog (Carantoc)

St. Cathan

St. Ceitho

St. Celynen

St. Cenydd

St. Cewydd

St. Cian

St. Clether ap Brychan

St. Clydog

St. Clydwyn ap Brychan

St. Crallo

St. Cwyllog

St. Cybi

St. Cynfarch

St. Cyngar

St. Cynidr

St. Cynllo

St. David

St. Degyman

St. Deiniol

St. Derfel Gadarn

St. Dogmael

St. Dwywe

St. Dyfnog

St. Dyfodwg

St. Dyfrig (Dubricius)

St. Eigrad

St. Eilian

St. Einion Frenin

St. Elaeth

St. Ailbe (Elvis)

St. Enoder

St. Enodoc

St. Ernin

St. Esyllt

St. Gildas

St. Govan

St. Gredifael

St. Guirec

St. Guron

St. Gwladys ferch Brychan

St. Gwrddelw

St. Gwrfyw

St. Gwyddfarch

St. Gwynard

St. Gwynllyw

St. Gwynnog

St. Henwyn

St. Hoel

St. Ilar

St. Isan

St. Isfael

St. Llechid

St. Llibio

St. Llwchalarn

St. Llyr

St. Maddern

St. Maglor

St. Maelog

St. Materiana

St. Mechell

St. Meilig

St. Merryn

St. Meugan

St. Mewan

St. Morwenna

Ss. Mybbard and Mancus

St. Ninnoc

St. Non

St. Pabo

St. Padarn

St. Paul Aurelian

St. Peirio

St. Peris

St. Petroc

St. Sadwrn
St. Saeran
St. Samson
St. Seiriol
St. Sulien
St. Tanwg
St. Tathan
St. Tathana
St. Tecwyn
St. Tegai
St. Teilo
St. Teulyddog
St. Tewdric
St. Trillo
St. Tudglyd
St. Tudno
St. Tudwal
St. Tudy
St. Twrog
St. Tydecho
St. Tyfaelog
St. Tyneio
St. Ufelwy

Seventh Century
St. Aelhaearn
St. Aerdeyrn
St. Beuno
St. Bodfan
St. Cadwaladr
St. Collen
St. Curig

St. Cwyfan
St. Cynfarwy
St. Dunod
St. Egwad
St. Eleri
St. Euddogwy (Oudoceus)
St. Eugrad
St. Gelert
St. Grwst
St. Gwenfrewy (Winifride)
St. Gwenllwyfo
St. Iestyn
St. Llily
St. Llwchaiarn
St. Madoc
St. Malo
St. Melangell
St. Tenoi
St. Tysilio
St. Winnoc

Eighth Century
St. Dominica
St. Gwbert
St. Urith

Unknown Date (Pre-Schism)
St. Ceneu
St. Ciwa
St. Clydai
St. Clydyn
St. Cowdra

St. Cristiolus

St. Cwyfen

St. Cynbryd

St. Cynddilig

St. Cynfab

St. Cynhafal

St. Cynwyl

St. Cywair

St. Deifer

St. Dilwar

St. Dona

St. Dyfnan

St. Dyvan

St. Edwen

St. Eigion

St. Elfan

St. Elli

St. Elwad

St. Elyw

St. Ewryd

St. Fidalis

St. Gallgo

St. Gistilian

St. Gofor

St. Gurthiern

St. Gwynan

St. Gwynhoedl

St. Gwynin

St. Gwenfaen

St. Gwenhiw

St. Gwenlleu

St. Gwenog

St. Gwrda

St. Gwrnerth

St. Gwrthwl

St. Gwyddelan

St. Hychan

St. Idloes

St. Illog

St. Issui

St. Llawddog

St. Llwelyn

St. Llwni

St. Llwydian

St. Llyr

St. Machraith

St. Maelrhys

St. Maethlu

St. Maidoc

St. Meddwid

St. Medwy

St. Meirion

St. Melyd

St. Mordeyrn

St. Morhairn

St. Mwrog

St. Mylling

St. Mynver

St. Noethan

St. Owen

St. Rhediw

St. Rhian

St. Rhuddlad

St. Rhychwyn

St. Sannan

St. Sawyl

St. Tegla

St. Teuderius

St. Trunio

St. Tudur

St. Tyfriog

St. Tygwy

St. Urw

St. Ylehed

APPENDIX 2

Approximate Locations of Early Christian Sites as Shown on a Modern Map of Wales[87]

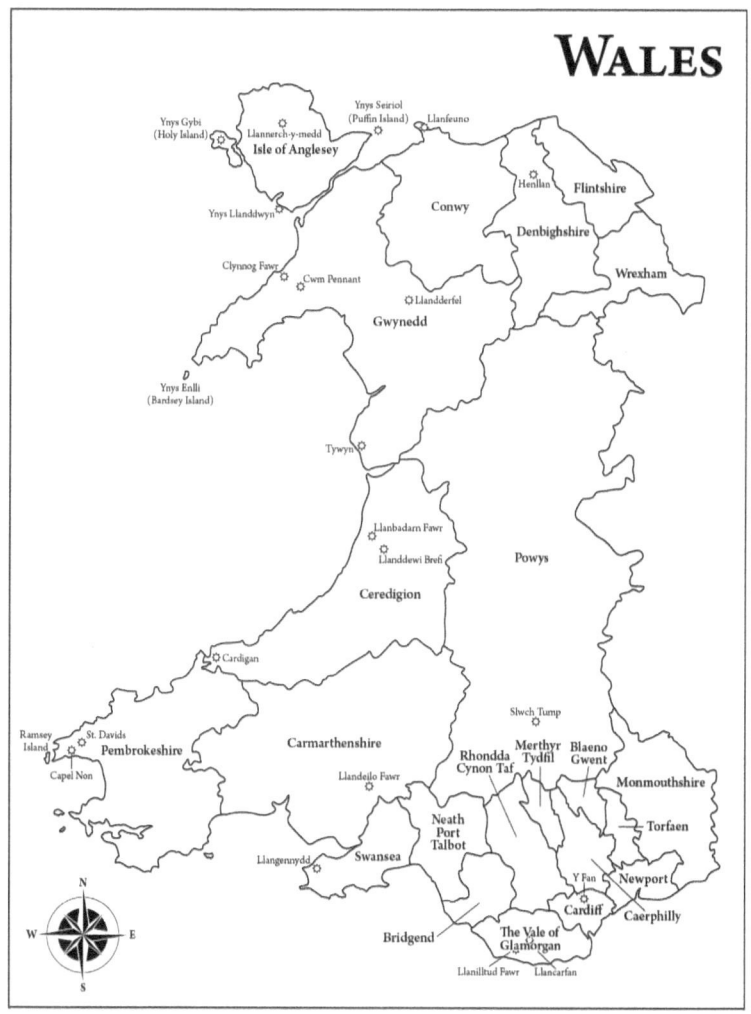

87   https://d-maps.com/carte.php?num_car=18291&lang=en.

APPENDIX 3

A Brief Guide to Welsh Pronunciation

As strange as many Welsh spellings may appear to the English speaker, it is helpful to understand that, unlike English, Welsh orthography is largely phonetic. As is the case with all languages, there are of course exceptions, but generally words are pronounced the way they are spelled. There are no silent letters in Welsh, and every letter is actually pronounced, regardless of how difficult this may appear to be—the only exception being diphthongs. The largest handicap to pronouncing Welsh names and words is the fact that several letters have different values in Welsh, as opposed to English. Keep in mind, though, that the sounds certain letters make in Welsh are far more consistent than in English. For example, the letter *c* in English can be pronounced as a *k* or as an *s* (and sometimes in other ways when combined with other letters). In Welsh a *c* is invariably pronounced as a *k*. There is no ambiguity.

Below is a general guideline for pronouncing letters in the Welsh alphabet.

Vowels

a—short as in English *cat*

e—as in English *bet*

i—usually as in *pin,* but sometimes as the *ee* in *seem*

o—usually as in *pot,* but sometimes as in *toe*

u—as the *ee* in *beet*

w—usually as the *oo* in *boot,* but sometimes as the *u* in *pull*

y—usually as the *u* in *run,* but sometimes as the *i* in *hit*

Consonants

b—same as in English

c—hard, as in English *cat;* never soft like English *city*

ch—as in Scottish *loch*

d—same as in English

dd—as the voiced *th* in English *there*

f—as the *v* in English *van*

ff—as the *f* in English *fan*

g—as in English *good*

ng—as in English *ring*

h—same as in English *house;* never silent like English *honest*

j—same as English (but only used in loanwords)

l—same as in English

ll—no English equivalent; it is made with the tongue in the *l* position and with air pushed through either side of the tongue, unvoiced; phonetic symbol ɬ

m—same as in English

n—same as in English

p—same as in English

ph—same as *ph* in English *phantom*

r—same as in English except rolled

rh—pronounced as though reversed, *hr,* with *h* sound preceding *r*

s—same as in English

si—same as *sh* in English *shall*

t—same as in English

th—same as the voiceless *th* in English *think* (as opposed to the voiced *dd*)

Diphthongs

ae, ai, au—all pronounced as the *y* in *my* or as the *igh* in *night*

aw—pronounced as the *ow* in *how*

ei, eu—pronounced as the *ay* in *day*

ew—no exact English equivalent but something like an exaggerated aristocratic *oh;* Welsh *Dewi* sounds very like how a young English-speaking child might pronounce *Derry* when they haven't learned to pronounce *r* correctly

oe, oi—pronounced as the *oy* in *boy*

ow—same as in English *brown*

wy—pronounced similar to the *ou* in French *oui* or *ui* in English *quit*

yw, iw—pronounced as the *ui* in *fluid*

Note that the Welsh alphabet does not contain the letters *k, q, v, x,* or *z.*

Syllabic Stress

As with any language, there can be many exceptions to the rule, but most polysyllabic words in Welsh have the stress on the penultimate (next-to-last) syllable. This means that most two-syllable words stress the first syllable and most three-syllable words stress the second syllable, etc. Two exceptions in this book are *Dwynwen* (**doo**-in-win) and *Eiliwedd* (**ay**-li-weth), both of which have the stress on the first syllable.

BIBLIOGRAPHY

Introduction

Anonymous. "Saint Winifred and Her Holy Spring." Orthodox Christianity. November 15, 2010. https://orthochristian.com/42777.html.

Baring-Gould, Sabine. *The Lives of the British Saints.* Vol. 4. The Honourable Society of Cymmrodorion, 1913.

Baring-Gould, Sabine, and John Fisher. *The Lives of the British Saints.* Vol. 2. The Honourable Society of Cymmrodorion, 1908.

Burke, Tony. "List of the Apostles and Disciples, by Pseudo-Hippolytus of Thebes." *e-Clavis: Christian Apocrypha.* Accessed October 17, 2024. https://www.nasscal.com/e-clavis-christian-apocrypha/list-of-the-apostles-and-disciples-by-pseudo-hippolytus-of-thebes/.

Clark, James G. *The Dissolution of the Monasteries: A New History.* Yale University Press, 2021.

Davies, J. B. *The Saints of Wales.* Catholic Truth Society, 1969.

Davies, Oliver. *Celtic Christianity in Early Medieval Wales.* University of Wales Press, 1996.

Geoffrey of Monmouth. *Histories of the Kings of Britain.* Translated by Sebastian Evans. https://sacred-texts.com/neu/eng/gem/gem05.htm.

Griffin, Justin E. *Glastonbury and the Grail.* McFarland, 2012.

Hutchison-Hall, John (Ellsworth). *Orthodox Saints of the British Isles.* 4 vols. Eadfrith Press, 2017.

Jones, David Ceri, Barry J. Lewis, Madeleine Gray, and D. Densil Morgan. *A History of Christianity in Wales.* University of Wales Press, 2022.

Lapa, Dmitry. "Venerable Beuno, Abbot of Clynnog Fawr in Wales." Orthodox Christianity. May 4, 2015. https://orthochristian.com/79097.html.

Lewis, Matt. "Lost Literature: Why Most English Texts Didn't Survive the Middle Ages." History Hit. October 1, 2022. https://www.historyhit.com/culture/lost-english-medieval-manuscripts/.

Morgan, Gerald. *In Pursuit of Saint David.* Y Lolfa, 2017.

Morgan, Richard Williams. *St. Paul in Britain.* Marshall Press, 1861.

Tertullian. "An Answer to the Jews." In *The Complete Works of Tertullian.* Translated by Philip Schaff. Kindle, 2016.

Earliest Welsh Saints: First–Fourth Centuries

Griffin, Justin E. *Glastonbury and the Grail.* McFarland, 2012.

Hutchison-Hall, John (Ellsworth). *Orthodox Saints of the British Isles.* 4 vols. Eadfrith Press, 2017.

Jones, David Ceri, Barry J. Lewis, Madeleine Gray, and D. Densil Morgan. *A History of Christianity in Wales.* University of Wales Press, 2022.

Morgan, Richard Williams. *St. Paul in Britain.* Marshall Press, 1861.

Pennick, Nigel. *The Celtic Saints.* Sterling Publishing, 1997.

Golden Age of Saints: Fifth Century

Anonymous. "Life of St. Illtud." *Lives of the Cambro British Saints.* Welsh Manuscript Society, 1853. https://www.celticchristianity.infinitesoulutions.com/books/Vita_Saint_Illtyd.pdf.

Davies, J. B. *The Saints of Wales.* Catholic Truth Society, 1969.

Doble, D. H. *Lives of the Welsh Saints.* University of Wales Press, 2013.

Lapa, Dmitry. "Holy Martyr Nectan of Hartland." Orthodox Christianity. June 26, 2015. https://orthochristian.com/80252.html.

Rees, William Jenkins. *Lives of the Cambro Saints.* Welsh Manuscript Society, 1853.

Spencer, Ray. *A Guide to the Saints of Wales and the West Country.* Llanerch Press, 1991.

Golden Age of Saints: Sixth Century

Catholic.net. "St. Paul Aurelian." https://catholic.net/op/articles/2775/cat/1205/st-paul-aurelian.html.

Davis, Paul. *Sacred Springs: In Search of the Holy Wells and Spas of Wales.* Blorenge Books, 2003.

EWTN. "St. Gildas the Wise." https://www.ewtn.com/catholicism/saints/gildas-the-wise-590.

Lapa, Dmitry. "Holy Heirarch David, Patron Saint of Wales." Orthodox Christianity. March 14, 2014. https://orthochristian.com/69157.html.

Lapa, Dmitry. "Saint Samson of Dol." Orthodox Christianity. August 10, 2017. https://orthochristian.com/105687.html.

Lapa, Dmitry. "Venerable Cadfan of Bardsey in Wales." Orthodox Christianity. November 14, 2016. https://orthochristian.com/98598.html.

Morgan, Gerald. *In Pursuit of Saint David*. Y Lolfa, 2017.

Spencer, Ray. *A Guide to the Saints of Wales and the West Country*. Llanerch Press, 1991.

Stanton, Richard. *A Menology of England and Wales*. Burns & Oates, 1892.

Sterling, Olivia. *St. David of Wales*. Privately published, 2024.

Taylor, Thomas. *Life of St. Samson of Dol*. Macmillan, 1925.

Golden Age of Saints: Seventh Century

Davies, J. B. *The Saints of Wales*. Catholic Truth Society, 1969.

Davis, Paul. *Sacred Springs: In Search of the Holy Wells and Spas of Wales*. Blorenge Books, 2003.

McLees, Nectaria. "Melangell with a Thousand Angels." Orthodox Christianity. June 9, 2014. https://orthochristian.com/71372.html.

New Advent. "St. Winefride." https://www.newadvent.org/cathen/15656a.htm.

Well Hopper. "Ffynnon Cwm Ewyn (Iewyn), Llangynog." https://wellhopper .wales/2013/08/21/ffynnon-cwm-ewyn-iewyn-llangynog/.

ABOUT THE AUTHOR

OSWIN CRATON WAS BORN AND grew up in Alabama but currently lives in Indiana. He is the author of *Holy Fools* (Ancient Faith Publishing, 2024) and also of *A Journey of Fear and Joy*, which is the story of his journey to Orthodoxy from a fundamentalist Protestant background. He is known in the music world under his birth name, John, and as a composer of classical music has written a number of ballets, operas, concertos, and other orchestral and chamber works that have been performed internationally. He is a member of All Saints Orthodox Church in Bloomington, Indiana. His patron saint is St. Oswin of Deira.

We hope you have enjoyed and benefited from this book. Your financial support makes it possible to continue our nonprofit ministry both in print and online. Because the proceeds from our book sales only partially cover the costs of operating **Ancient Faith Publishing** and **Ancient Faith Radio,** we greatly appreciate the generosity of our readers and listeners. Donations are tax deductible and can be made at **www.ancientfaith.com.**

To view our other publications,
please visit our website:
store.ancientfaith.com

Bringing you Orthodox Christian music, readings,
prayers, teaching, and podcasts 24 hours a day since 2004 at
www.ancientfaith.com

www.ingramcontent.com/pod-product-compliance
Lightning Source LLC
Chambersburg PA
CBHW031427120626
46545CB00006B/2308